PRAISE FOR

CALLED BACK TO WHO YOU ARE

I0605476

Whitney's words are uniquely and powerfully anointed. As you read this book, you won't be met by only her tender compassion but her strong conviction to unearthing the true meaning and beauty of God's Word. In a world that is constantly calling for your attention elsewhere, find reminders of God's peace and presence on these pages.

TARA SUN, AUTHOR OF *SURRENDER YOUR STORY* AND *OVERBOOKED AND OVERWHELMED*; PODCAST HOST, *TRUTH TALKS WITH TARA*

The way Whitney Lowe goes to bat for God's character in this book, pleading on His behalf for those who don't realize how intently He seeks and pursues us, is incredible. Her invitation to walk through her journey, showcasing how He has relentlessly drawn her back while simultaneously pointing us to His pursuit in our own lives, will leave you in awe of the kindness of God.

MARIELA ROSARIO, AUTHOR; FOUNDER, SHE SPEAKS FIRE

I was drawn into *Called Back to Who You Are* from the beginning and excitedly anticipated when I could sit down and continue reading. Whitney takes us on a Scripture-soaked journey of God's incredible love for us reflected in His relentless pursuit of us. She offers a beautiful blend of biblical knowledge with storytelling and the honesty of her own faith journey. Whitney is a faithful and trusted source to learn from. Her words captured my attention and often moved me to tears. I love this book; it is now a favorite of mine!

KARA STOUT, AUTHOR; WIFE; MOM

Whitney Lowe has taken a deep dive into Scripture's teaching about God's gracious, loving pursuit of us—and in doing so, she shows how our hearts can be radically transformed as we embrace who the Lord created us to be.

GREG AND ERIN SMALLEY, COUNSELORS; AUTHORS; SPEAKERS

Called Back to Who You Are is a tender, truth-filled homecoming for every heart that's felt lost in the wild. With poetic clarity and deep spiritual insight, Whitney Lowe gently leads us back to the love of God and the truth of who we've always been. Her words don't just inspire, they anchor. This book is a healing companion for the ones learning to live loved.

CASSANDRA SPEER, BESTSELLING AUTHOR; BIBLE TEACHER; PODCAST HOST, *HARD & HOLY*; VICE PRESIDENT, HER TRUE WORTH

Called Back to Who You Are is a compelling testimony to God's relentless pursuit of our hearts, even when we distance ourselves. Whitney Lowe offers readers a profound invitation to see their lives through the lens of God's divine love rather than the world's lies and rediscover their identities according to God's Word. This book will fortify your faith, clarify your understanding of God's character, and affirm your identity as one passionately and persistently loved by the Lord. Whitney's story resonates because it calls to our greatest place of need: to be known and loved by our Creator.

CHRISTINA CRENSHAW, PHD, AUTHOR; SPEAKER; PROFESSOR

CALLED BACK TO WHO YOU ARE

WHO YOU ARE CALLED BACK TO

FINDING YOURSELF IN THE WILD, PURSUING LOVE OF GOD

WHITNEY LOWE

ZONDERVAN BOOKS

Called Back to Who You Are
Copyright © 2026 by Whitney Lowe

Published by Zondervan, 3950 Sparks Drive SE, Suite 101, Grand Rapids, MI 49546, USA. Zondervan is a registered trademark of The Zondervan Corporation, L.L.C., a wholly owned subsidiary of HarperCollins Christian Publishing, Inc.

Requests for information should be addressed to customercare@harpercollins.com.

Zondervan titles may be purchased in bulk for educational, business, fundraising, or sales promotional use. For information, please email SpecialMarkets@Zondervan.com.

Library of Congress Cataloging-in-Publication Data

Names: Lowe, Whitney, 1992- author.
Title: Called back to who you are : finding yourself in the wild, pursuing love of God / Whitney Lowe.
Description: Grand Rapids, Michigan : Zondervan Books, [2026] | Includes bibliographical references.
Identifiers: LCCN 2025001932 (print) | LCCN 2025001933 (ebook) | ISBN 9780310367970 (trade paperback) | ISBN 9780310367987 (ebook) | ISBN 9780310367994 (audio)
Subjects: LCSH: God (Christianity)—Love. | Love—Religious aspects—Christianity. | Christian life.
Classification: LCC BT140 .L687 2025 (print) | LCC BT140 (ebook) | DDC 231/.6—dc23/eng/20250328
LC record available at https://lccn.loc.gov/2025001932
LC ebook record available at https://lccn.loc.gov/2025001933

Unless otherwise noted, Scripture quotations are taken from The Holy Bible, New International Version®, NIV®. Copyright © 1973, 1978, 1984, 2011 by Biblica, Inc.® Used by permission of Zondervan. All rights reserved worldwide. www.Zondervan.com. The "NIV" and "New International Version" are trademarks registered in the United States Patent and Trademark Office by Biblica, Inc.®

Scripture quotations marked ESV are taken from the ESV® Bible (The Holy Bible, English Standard Version®). Copyright © 2001 by Crossway, a publishing ministry of Good News Publishers. Used by permission. All rights reserved.

Scripture quotations marked NASB are taken from the (NASB®) New American Standard Bible®. Copyright © 1960, 1971, 1977, 1995, 2020 by The Lockman Foundation. Used by permission. All rights reserved. www.lockman.org.

Scripture quotations marked NLT are taken from the Holy Bible, New Living Translation. Copyright © 1996, 2004, 2015 by Tyndale House Foundation. Used by permission of Tyndale House Publishers, Inc., Carol Stream, Illinois 60188. All rights reserved.

Scripture quotations marked NRSV are taken from the New Revised Standard Version Bible. Copyright © 1989 National Council of the Churches of Christ in the United States of America. Used by permission. All rights reserved.

Any internet addresses (websites, blogs, etc.) and telephone numbers in this book are offered as a resource. They are not intended in any way to be or imply an endorsement by Zondervan, nor does Zondervan vouch for the content of these sites and numbers for the life of this book.

All rights reserved. No part of this publication may be reproduced, stored in a retrieval system, or transmitted in any form or by any means—electronic, mechanical, photocopy, recording, or any other—except for brief quotations in printed reviews, without the prior permission of the publisher.

Published in association with The Bindery Agency, www.TheBinderyAgency.com.

Without limiting the exclusive rights of any author, contributor or the publisher of this publication, any unauthorized use of this publication to train generative artificial intelligence (AI) technologies is expressly prohibited. HarperCollins also exercise their rights under Article 4(3) of the Digital Single Market Directive 2019/790 and expressly reserve this publication from the text and data mining exception.

HarperCollins Publishers, Macken House, 39/40 Mayor Street Upper, Dublin 1, D01 C9W8, Ireland (https://www.harpercollins.com)

Cover illustration: Irina Davydenko / iStockphoto
Interior design: Emily Ghattas

Printed in the United States of America

25 26 27 28 29 LBC 5 4 3 2 1

To Tanner.

You live out the love that doesn't give up.

CONTENTS

INTRODUCTION

I hadn't slept in weeks. You'd think it was because of the jet lag—I had just arrived in Istanbul—and because of the ten-hour time difference, it was to a degree. But my insomnia had plagued me well before I got on that plane. It was the summer of 2014, and my college graduation had happened just a month earlier, wrapping up a rich, beautiful, excruciating, and complicated four years of my life. Unfortunately, the last two adjectives in that list best described my senior year, and I was still reeling from the punches, many thrown by my own arm and landed with my own fist.

In what I fear was another clichéd attempt by a lost twentysomething to find herself, I signed up through my school to go to Turkey to work with refugees that summer. At the time, the Syrian refugee crisis was near its peak, and Turkey was inundated by desperate people fleeing impossible situations. As a lifelong Christian who had not been living like one, I was trying to reconnect with God by doing something that seemed godly in hopes that I would find some sure footing after a season of disorientation.

In my junior year of college, I slowly drifted into alignment with the cultural narratives that led me to believe I was having fun, that living life to the fullest meant trading stories about drunken nights with friends—including many who didn't care all that much about me—and living for the memories I wouldn't actually remember. For a while, this lifestyle was exhilarating, offering me a kind of freedom I thought I wanted. And it allowed me to turn away from the questions about my faith that deeply troubled me and that I was unable to answer: Why was the church so broken? And why was there so much suffering in the world? These were more than philosophical questions, though; they turned into doubts about my faith and then left me doubting that God cared about me personally and had truly designed me with a purpose. My doubts culminated in a slow yet forceful drift from addressing these tough questions and from God Himself and directly toward a special type of hedonism—despite knowing better, I chose to stop caring and decided to "live" instead. After all, fun can drown out the jet-engine roar of an existential crisis, at least for a time. But it ultimately delivered nothing more than escape and shallow enjoyment. Of course I felt distant from God and confused about who I was. Once my identity was no longer tied to the solid ground I had always found in my relationship with Jesus, I was just out there flailing like one of those used-car-lot balloon people. I was empty, chaotic, and afraid.

When your identity isn't tethered to truth, lies tether themselves to *you*. Once you start to doubt that God made you with a purpose, you start to doubt that He cares about you at all. If He doesn't care about you on a personal level, you can do what you want. "Is He even real? Why would I do what He says?" we ask. The logic of godlessness cycles through itself, seemingly proving its premises and driving you further away the longer you entertain it.

Before I knew it, this lifelong Christian from a stable and (mostly) healthy family with significant economic and academic privilege and very few excuses had a much longer rap sheet than I'd ever imagined. I didn't ask darkness to take over my life, but I was certainly running from the light. I didn't want to be exposed, but I was struggling with what felt like the truth—that I was worthless and unlovable—so I fell deeper into the trap. Since I was so dead set on running from God, where else could I possibly end up but in the horrible pit mentioned in Psalm 40?

During that time, I lost myself and found more darkness within me than I ever knew. Maybe you'll hear a little of your story somewhere in this list too:

- I reduced my goals and value to revolve around the physical, the tangible, the visible.
- I clung to numbness. If it helped me short-circuit a sense of peace or belonging, I was in. Drinking, calorie counting, gossiping, and reckless spending—these were just a few of the ways I manufactured a high that enabled me to continue pretending I was happy and didn't really need God.

- I treated human beings (some of whom remain the most important people in my life) as characters in my story instead of image bearers of a holy God.

While these statements describe my story—my testimony, if you will—at least one (if not all) can apply to most sins. Sin demands that we fixate on the physical and self-medicate to find temporary relief. It always leads us to objectify either ourselves or others, because it always minimizes the image of God within us. It makes sense that I was completely lost. Not only was I using others, but I frequently found myself defenseless against the dysfunction in others, so the hurt proliferated. Have you been there too?

By the time I made it to Istanbul, I was keenly aware that something—everything, perhaps—was wrong and had been for some time. The acute insomnia I was suffering only made that awareness more pronounced. One of God's "backward graces" to me is that I cannot rest when my soul needs maintenance; there is no filing away my problems. Immediate action required! Another backward grace in Istanbul was that the Wi-Fi was spotty and every TV channel was in Turkish or Russian, so I found myself with no easy distractions in the early hours of the morning. It was me and a lot of tears.

It was also me and the presence of a God who wanted me back, a God who hated to see me crying over sin He had already defeated. A God who hated the lies I believed, the things I had done, and the things that had been done to me, enough to bear their full burden on my behalf. In a random Airbnb in the

Cihangir neighborhood of Istanbul, with the haunting Islamic call to prayer cutting through the dark morning hours, God was there.

On that very first morning, unadjusted to the ten-hour time difference, I found myself wide awake at two, heart racing and feeling heavy all at once. I tossed and turned in bed for a while, then I gave up and went to the living room and turned on the light. I scoured the bookshelves for a book—any book—that wasn't in Turkish, but to no avail. I picked up the newspaper and tried to translate as many Turkish words as I knew. I couldn't find an adequate distraction from the deep fear and pain I felt, no matter how hard I tried.

I finally caved and opened the only book I had brought with me—my Bible. I had the overwhelming feeling that I needed to open it to the book of Hosea (a book I had barely read, despite majoring in religious studies). I am not sure I have an explanation for this feeling, apart from the pure and gracious leading of the Holy Spirit trying to get through to my stubborn heart. Hosea, one of the minor prophets in the Old Testament, was a man living in the eighth century BC whom God called to marry a woman named Gomer. Gomer is traditionally understood to be a prostitute, but scholars aren't sure.[1] Regardless, Gomer was not faithful to her marriage covenant with Hosea. And that is the whole point: This book of the Bible shows us in stark relief how our pursuit of false gods breaks the heart of the true One. More than that, the book of Hosea shows us the lengths to which our holy God will go to pursue and win back His beloved people, even today.

I will never forget the terror, warmth, and profound feeling of being seen I experienced when reading Hosea 2. The chapter starts with a list of wrongs and all the things Gomer deserved punishment for. This provides a metaphor for Israel's failure to be faithful to God, so the indictment is as heavy as you'd expect:

> "I will ruin her vines and her fig trees,
> which she said were her pay from her lovers;
> I will make them a thicket,
> and wild animals will devour them." (Hosea 2:12)

I felt those words deeply. I knew they could have been written for me. I knew God was mad at what I had done; I had judgment coming, and deservedly so. I wept and I wept, but I kept reading.

Then came verse 14:

> "Therefore I am now going to allure her;
> I will lead her into the wilderness
> and speak tenderly to her."

"Oh!" I said upon reading the stark change in tone.

Instead of giving full vent to the righteous, justified fury of a scorned husband, God chooses something different. He chooses tenderness. God wants to get His beloved away from the counterfeit lovers long enough for her to hear Him clearly. Where He could choose to reprimand, He chooses to allure.

God led me to this passage in the dark of that morning. Over the next weeks, I found myself up before dawn each day, returning to the book of Hosea and weeping my way through its pages. There I was, traveling with three other students but otherwise by myself in a foreign country. By day, I served lunch to families of refugees and taught English to displaced parents doing everything they could to make a way for their children. The experience was hard, and it would have been hard even if I had been in a great spot emotionally and spiritually. Getting caught up in my coping mechanisms and fixating on my own insecurities for the past few years made it all the more painful, as I was forced to acknowledge that I had very little to offer the people I was allegedly there to serve. I was in daily situations that led me to contend with deep feelings of loneliness, fear, and worthlessness. God drew me into a desert of my own, but God (although He would certainly hold me accountable for my actions) did not intend to chastise and ridicule me. God knew the blinding pain, ignorance, and genuine deception behind so many of my terrible choices. He had not given up on me.

In reading Hosea, I suddenly and clearly saw that God had been pursuing me—unfaithful though I was and disgraceful though I felt—that whole time. This moment changed everything for me. The entire trajectory of my life shifted in that singular moment of realizing that the God of the universe was running after me!

The book of Hosea has been special to me ever since.

Hosea is among the most evocative and complex pictures of God's pursuit in the Bible, but it's not the only one. Once you start to look (and together, we will), you will see that from the very beginning, God takes the burden of our covenant on Himself when we fail. His plan has always accounted for our frailty. Does this mean we should persist in rebellion, taking this "reckless" love for granted? No! This profound, unnatural, won't-give-up grace is what drives us to repentance. When we finally trust the heart of this God who condescends to pursue us, we stop running (Romans 6:1–4, my rough paraphrase).

Realizing that God would never give up on me—unfaithful and rebellious and without excuse though I was—changed everything for me. I think it will change everything for you too. In the world we live in, God is often seen as distant and uninvolved. When we mess up or walk through seasons of rebellion, we believe God has rejected us, or at least lost interest. Maybe we think God is so disappointed in us that we must wait until we've improved our proverbial report card before He will feel near again. At minimum He's just a little too busy to be actively interested in our day-to-day.

Maybe you've heard the expression "God is a gentleman," ultimately meant to affirm that we have free will as humans and that God won't force us to submit to His will. I hate that expression. While God does not deprive us of free will, He is no gentleman. He isn't a man at all. Gentlemen eventually tire of waiting and pursuing. Gentlemen, though polite, are motivated by their own desires and are ultimately invested in their own benefit as much as (or more than) yours. Politeness is great, but it's not the same as sacrificial, long-suffering, unconditional love. God is infinite and merciful, and He is infinitely merciful. God does not move on to the next person after we've rejected Him enough times. God stays close through the heartbreak He knows we will experience when we choose distance from Him, even though He knows it will break His heart too.

God honors free will, but He is not so petty and weak that our rejection deactivates His love. You simply *can't* deactivate the Love that dies on our behalf. That Love sticks around; that Love never stops pursuing the flourishing of its beloved.

If you don't understand how deeply you are wanted by the God of the universe, you will go through life feeling less-than. There is no one who will maintain a more vehement interest in you than your Creator. You must understand your identity in light of God's desire for you. If you don't see God's pursuit, you can't fully conceive of His love. If you don't experience the fullness of His love, you will not accurately show that love to others.

In this book, I want to open your eyes to all the ways that the God of the universe is running after you at full speed, bounding over hills without stumbling or faltering. First, we will dig into what it means theologically to be pursued by God, and we will ground our understanding in Scripture. Then we will discuss the implications of that pursuit: "What does it mean for my life if He will never stop seeking me?" We will end with an exploration of how we should respond to God's pursuit by embodying that truth in our own lives. Throughout it all, I want you to look back at your story, unearthing the ways God has consistently led you into goodness or guided you back into peace. Even if you sometimes cried out, "God, where are You?" Even if His pursuit sometimes felt painful.

In looking at the ways God pursues us—even in our least deserving states and our most shameful rebellions—we will find the solid rock of His goodness on which we can stake our entire identity. We will find the quiet waters and green pastures of Psalm 23, where we can encounter true rest that shows us that we are completely safe and adored. In that place of rest, we will find our very souls reinvigorated, like an internal revival is taking place.

In recent years, many Christians (for good reason) have prayed for God to bring revival: in our churches, in our nation, in our world. To these Christians, revival looks like people repenting of their sins and returning to Jesus by the thousands. Secondarily (and necessarily), they want to see our collective moral compass restored and to see peace prevail. Finally, they want to experience miracles and the supernatural power of God at work through revival. I know because I'm one of them.

But here's what I think we have been missing: Large-scale revival has to start with internal revival in individual hearts that are convinced God is desperately seeking them. Revival will come only when we find true rest in Him. Revival has always been at its core an act of receiving God's very real, very relentless pursuit of His people.

Dwelling on God's pursuit brought the Bible to life for me. Those early morning hours in Turkey studying Hosea took me on a journey through every page of the Bible over the following years. I discovered that God's pursuit of His people—of us, of *you*—is on every single page. It brought me to my knees in worship and wonder as I uncovered more and more evidence of His strength, His kindness, and His power. God's pursuit of His own creation sets Him apart from other gods and religions:

He deserves glory and worship, yet when He is most justified to punish, He chooses to become flesh, with all its weaknesses, and draw near to *us* (John 1:14). An almighty, awesome God chooses to stoop low and dignify us with His effort and consistency. It's breathtaking.

What if, just for a little while, you stop looking at your shame or disappointment or brokenness and start looking at all God has done for you *in spite of* it? What if, for the next few chapters, you choose to believe against all reason that the God of the universe desperately wants to be close to you? What if, just for now, you let yourself believe that His goodness and mercy are following you all the days of your life, and that He is waiting for you to stop running long enough to receive them? Give it a shot.

God has pursued your heart since the moment He made it, friend. This is where revival happens. It changes everything.

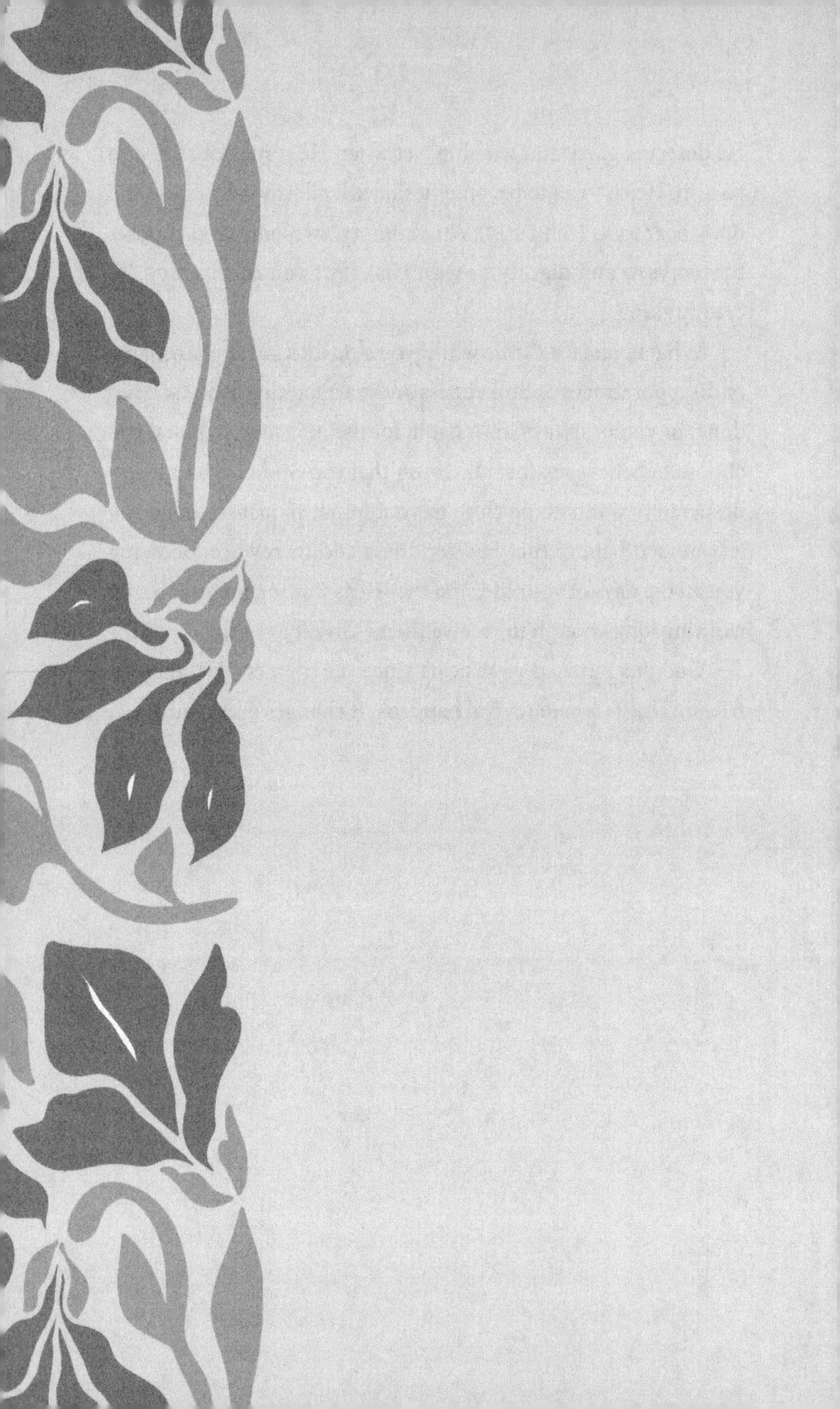

PART 1

GOD, OUR PURSUER

WHAT DOES IT MEAN, BIBLICALLY AND THEOLOGICALLY, TO BE PURSUED BY GOD?

The Word became flesh and made his dwelling among us. We have seen his glory, the glory of the one and only Son, who came from the Father, full of grace and truth. (John 1:14)

To understand what God's pursuit looks like, we must track God's relationship with His people from the very beginning. In this section, I share the basis for the concept of divine pursuit so that together we can marvel at how good He is and has always been. By looking at the lengths to which He has gone for His people throughout Scripture, you will get a clearer picture of what He invites you into this very day.

CHAPTER 1

SURELY HIS GOODNESS WILL FOLLOW ME

As a religious studies major at Westmont College in sunny Santa Barbara, California, I sat in my upper-division classes often with just five to ten other students gathered around a conference table. The lecture looked more like a guided discussion with plenty of time to explore complex topics and ask hard questions. Aside from how obvious it was when I came to class unprepared (which was too often), I loved it. I loved getting to hear the surprisingly wide variety of perspectives brought to the table by ostensibly evangelical Christian students.

In one of my favorite classes, which was on the theology of human sexuality, one of my classmates wept over her textbook, recounting abuse that had taken place in her own life. Earlier in the class, someone else had brought up how God pursues us. She gestured to him and said, "I hate that terminology. Pursuit is violent. Pursuit implies a hunt. After what I've been through, I honestly cannot even allow myself to imagine God hunting me down like a wounded animal."

Whoa. This wasn't just some desire to take offense, for which others so often criticize my generation (often accompanied by the pejorative title of "snowflake"). Looking at the sincere pain in her eyes, I could tell she was in the midst of processing very real trauma and very honest fear. One of my male classmates seemed unconvinced, even a little dismissive. Others were empathetic to the point of committing to avoid triggering terminology in future discussions. Although I truly felt for her and the hurt she carried, I couldn't turn from the language of pursuit, because the Bible continuously paints a picture of a God who pursues the humans He created. He seeks us out to save us from ourselves (even when we reject Him and run away).

Yes, wrapping our minds around God's pursuit is fraught and complex. Should that mean we avoid speaking about God in certain ways, particularly how Scripture speaks about God, in the interest of steering clear of all personal and cultural baggage and hurt? No. But we should seek to be thoughtful and precise when we tread on tender ground. With the image of God pursuing His people, it was clear to me that we *needed* to unpack the concept of divine pursuit, and do it well. A lot was at stake if we got it wrong, especially for my suffering classmate. I spent that entire semester pondering her objections, and although they weren't something we discussed at length again, my authentic interest in making sense of God's pursuit only grew.

If we seek to understand God's pursuit of us exclusively through the lens of the human experience, we will surely miss the holy gentleness and sacrificial love that are intrinsic to His pursuit.

So let's dig in. What does it *really* mean to be pursued by God?

Simply put, pursuit is desire moved to its feet.

God wants a relationship with us so deeply that He stands up from the throne and comes right down to earth to engage us, wherever we may be found. Surely His goodness does follow us (Psalm 23:6).

Theologians might tell you that the perfect love we see moving in and through the Trinity was so abundant and perfect that it overflowed into the massive act of creation. John Piper says it's "the nature of the fullness of the divine love to share itself."[1] I think that's true.

I wonder, though, if these lofty theological discussions sometimes brush over the part of Genesis 1 wherein God simply decides to create because *He wants to*: "Then God said, 'Let us make mankind in our image, in our likeness, so that they may rule over the fish in the sea and the birds in the sky, over the livestock and all the wild animals, and over all the creatures that move along the ground.' So God created mankind in his own image, in the image of God he created them; male and female he created them" (Genesis 1:26–27).

It's fascinating to compare the creation accounts in Genesis to other creation narratives from surrounding ancient Near

Eastern cultures, since we can assume these narratives are conversant with one another to some degree. In the Babylonian creation myth called the *Enuma Elish*, human beings are created in the wake of extreme violence among the gods so humans can do the labor that the gods don't want to do. Sumerian creation myths offer the same explanation: The gods are tired of working, and they need to create laborers "so that they can be freed from their toil."[2]

In stark contrast, Yahweh creates humans in the dignity of His own image to rule the way He rules. He doesn't need them to bear some burden He's tired of; He simply desires them to exist.

> "You are worthy, our Lord and God,
>   to receive glory and honor and power,
> for you created all things,
>   and *by your will* they were created
>   and have their being."
>
> (Revelation 4:11, emphasis added)

It's stunningly simple. God wanted humans, so He made them. God wanted you, so God brought you into existence. Creation itself is an act of pursuit.

If you're not convinced, let's look at the way He interacts with His image bearers once He forms them: He gives humans dominion over the rest of nature as an invitation to participate in the work of creation *alongside* Him. Through Adam and Eve, He establishes the first human family as a direct reflection of the inner workings of the Trinity itself, but also as a providential gift that man should not exist in solitude. Even after Adam and Eve directly defy the boundaries He set for their good, God comes to walk in the garden in the cool of the evening. Adam and Eve know the sounds of His footsteps well enough to hide from them, which implies that God walked often in the beautiful place He had given them. They live close enough to Him that He could pop by for a visit.

In response to their rebellion, God doesn't destroy them in His anger. He doesn't revoke His image from their nature in His disappointment. He doesn't banish them from His presence.

> The Lord God made garments of skin for Adam and his wife and clothed them. And the Lord God said, "The man has now become like one of us, knowing good and evil. He must not be allowed to reach out his hand and take also from the tree of life and eat, and live forever." So the Lord God banished him from the Garden of Eden to work the ground from which he had been taken. (Genesis 3:21–23)

For their own good and survival, God removes Adam and Eve from the place He had given them. Now that they know of good and evil, the worst-case scenario would be also eating from the tree of life, which confers eternal life. To have both knowledge and eternal life would crush them under the insurmountable burden that God alone is capable of bearing. By removing them from the garden, He thus protects them from an unending life of carrying the burden of knowing evil. He promises a Savior who will right all the wrongs their actions unleashed. He promises an end to all suffering. He goes even further: He doesn't just protect them from the eternal burden of evil, but He takes the burden on Himself so they can eventually live eternally in peace, joy, and freedom with Him. And then He follows them out of the garden and into the desert.

God does not revoke His presence from Adam and Eve. Why? Because He wants to be close to them.

He deals with their descendants in the same way. God chooses Abram, a childless man living in what we believe is now modern-day Iraq, to father the nation of Israel. He calls Abram out of his homeland and into a new one yet to be defined. He promises him children, despite Abram and his wife Sarai being well past the childbearing years.

In Genesis 15 we see God ratify His promises to Abram through a covenant ceremony. Abram (yet to be renamed Abraham) is commanded to bring multiple animals, cut them in half, and lay them down with a path between the pieces. He does so and falls into a deep sleep, after which we are told the following: "When the sun had set and darkness had fallen, a smoking firepot with a blazing torch appeared and passed between the pieces. On that day the LORD made a covenant with Abram" (Genesis 15:17–18). It's a weird story, for sure. I used to pass right over it, along with the other Old Testament accounts and commandments related to bloody sacrifices, whose significance seemed lost in the millennia between today and the times when these practices were commonplace. Cultural context is precisely what we need to understand how profound this moment is in Scripture.

What we witness in Genesis 15 has many parallels to a royal land grant ceremony, something that ancient audiences would have been familiar with, wherein a king (or individual with similar power) bestowed property upon the grantee in perpetuity, in exchange for their loyalty. During this ceremony in the ancient world of Abram, the animals were cut into two pieces and placed across from one another, as if to say (as we see in Jeremiah 34:18), "Let this be my fate if I renege on our covenant." In other words, they offered a visible, visceral image of the consequences of violating the terms of the covenant. As a final step, the two parties walked through the aisle created in this gruesome scene to complete the ceremony and enact the contract.

Go back and reread Genesis 15:12–17. Abram is *asleep*. God alone walks the bloody path. God alone commits to uphold the covenant. God, for no reason except His steadfast love for humans and His sovereignty, essentially says, "Let this be done to me if *either* of us breaks this covenant." Friend, God knows He isn't going to be the one to break it. He knows His own body will break to fulfill this covenant of love and commitment toward His people. Right there, in the first book of the Bible, God promises Himself to the relentless pursuit of broken, rebellious people.

Lest you believe that Abram is perfectly faithful and obedient to God's every command from this point forward, I want to point out that—on multiple occasions—Abram and Sarai's actions betray their lack of faith that these promises could ever be real. The *very next chapter* (Genesis 16) tells of the horrific abuse Hagar, Sarai's slave, endures to ensure this family has an heir. Sarai, impatient and unconvinced of God's provision, insists that Abram sleep with Hagar to get her pregnant. It works. After the fact, Sarai comes to the shocking realization that she is uncomfortable with this arrangement. She is entirely too jealous to have Hagar around, so she treats this young pregnant woman so poorly that Hagar flees into the desert. It's good to remember that the Bible is often descriptive and not necessarily prescriptive. Make no mistake: Abram and Sarai sin gravely in their treatment of Hagar.

But God pursues sweet Hagar. An angel of the Lord goes after her in the desert and makes sure she knows God has a big meaningful plan for her too. To make sure she knows she is not merely an accessory to the narrative of Abram and Sarai. To affirm the worth and dignity God implants in her: Hagar, the mother of Ishmael, technically outside the covenant God makes with His chosen people (Abram's descendants through Sarai, as God elucidates in Genesis 17). To Hagar, He is the God who sees her (Genesis 16:13) and goes after her to speak life over the future that looks dead and to speak promises of hope in her time of desperation. Yes, the road is hard, but Hagar—the slave far away from home—mothers a nation, just like Abram fathers one. God's pursuit is so much bigger than the categories we live by.

Sociologist and pastor Tony Campolo tells a story that perfectly illustrates God's category-breaking pursuit. One night, on a trip to Honolulu, Tony found himself in a rough part of town and seated in a grimy diner. It was 3:30 a.m., so he settled in with his coffee and a doughnut. Before long, a group of women (all sex workers) entered the diner for a quick break during their night shift. As he was preparing to leave, Tony overheard one of the women mention that it was her birthday the following day, and upon receiving a less-than-kind response from her companion, she added she'd never had a birthday party in her life. Upon overhearing this, Tony says he "made a decision." When the women left, Tony confirmed with the diner employees that the women came in every night around the same time. He found out that the woman's name was Agnes. He asked if he could return the following night with decorations and a cake to give Agnes the birthday party she had never experienced. The owner loved the idea.

The following night, Tony arrived at the diner and found that word had gotten out about Agnes's birthday party. He set up the decorations and directed the group to prepare for the big surprise when she arrived. As you can imagine, Agnes walked in and was stunned. She was so touched that when they lit the candles on the cake and sang "Happy Birthday," she wept openly. Wanting to savor every bit of the celebration, she asked if she could take the cake home. In that moment Pastor Campolo felt called to lead the whole group in a moment of prayer for Agnes, for every vulnerable woman in that room, and for the salvation of every soul who bore witness to that sacred celebration.

Tony recounts the diner owner's poignant reaction after he finished praying: "When I finished, Harry leaned over the counter and, with a trace of hostility in his voice, he said, 'Hey! You never told me you were a preacher. What kind of church do you belong to?' In one of those moments when just the right words came, I answered, 'I belong to a church that throws birthday parties for [sex workers] at 3:30 in the morning.'

"Harry waited a moment and then almost sneered as he answered, 'No you don't. There's no church like that. If there was, I'd join it. I'd join a church like that!'"[3]

See, we like to put people into categories: worthy, unworthy, good enough, too far gone. We act like Jesus is primarily concerned with the clean-cut kids who show up to church on Sunday and keep their sins quiet. In our own efforts to serve and to love—to pursue others—we often stop when it becomes inconvenient or uncomfortable, when we feel challenged by cross-cultural communication or socioeconomic differences or lifestyle choices gone bad.

God isn't like that. Yes, God pursues those of us who "look the part." But He doesn't stop there. God loves to go to the least likely person in the least likely place so He can lift up her chin, however bruised and battered, and speak dignity and value over her. He did it for Agnes, providing a celebration of her life in a diner at 3:30 a.m. He did it for Hagar, pregnant and discarded by the "good religious folks" to die in the desert. God is undeterred by the labels you claim (or labels others have designated for you) or the lifestyle you've embraced. Like the father in the parable of the prodigal son (Luke 15:11–32), He is running toward you with love in His eyes to set you free and bring you home.

God isn't done with Abraham either. Abraham (renamed when God promises to make him the father of many nations in Genesis 17) fathers Isaac, who fathers Jacob. Jacob, like his grandpa, finds himself renamed. He is now Israel, which means "struggles with God," a name that I find deeply relatable. Israel fathers twelve sons, who in turn father each of the twelve tribes of—you guessed it!—Israel. They sell their own brother Joseph into slavery in Egypt, and when a famine eventually strikes the land, that same brother waits for them there with power and resources to keep them alive. God's commitment to take care of Abraham's descendants consistently supersedes their failure to deserve it.

Joseph, now a leader in Egypt reconciling with his guilt-ridden brothers, explains the sovereignty of God and His power over and against the evil we commit in our moments of weakness: "'You intended to harm me, but God intended it for good to accomplish what is now being done, the saving of many lives. So then, don't be afraid. I will provide for you and your children.' And he reassured them and spoke kindly to them" (Genesis 50:20–21).

Enter Moses. You've heard of him, right? God places a Hebrew baby in the Egyptian courts, equipping him to navigate the cultures of both the oppressed and their oppressor. God disciplines him into a leader of integrity, through Moses's mistakes and through his years in the desert tending sheep. "I have indeed seen the misery of my people in Egypt. I have heard them crying out because of their slave drivers, and I am concerned about their suffering," God says (Exodus 3:7). God is so distressed by the suffering of His people that something has to be done. Moses is the guy for the job.

God sends Moses to free Israel, the nation God covenanted to Himself. He has to. He promised. Moses leaves his desert haven and heads right back into the mess to obey God and fight for the Israelites' freedom. Through Moses, God liberates His people from their oppressors and subsequently draws them into the wilderness, where their true freedom is found in dependence on Him.

It isn't a pretty story. Moses starts out terrified and resistant to the call God gives him. He is clumsy with his words and lacking in confidence. When he finally submits and goes back to Egypt, Pharaoh doesn't listen. Despite God offering many opportunities for him to free the Hebrew people of his own volition, he relents only after ten plagues wreak havoc on his people. Pharaoh's dogged commitment to slavery ultimately costs the Egyptians their firstborn sons, including Pharaoh's own. Even then, Pharaoh still changes his mind at the last minute and chases the Israelites all the way to the Red Sea, where God parts the waters for the Israelites but the Egyptian army meets its bitter end.

When God has to break us free from whatever bondage we're in, sometimes things get messy. When we insist on chains—whether we wear them or hold the keys—God will eventually just break them off.

When I was recovering from an eating disorder over the months after my work in Istanbul, at times I felt like I was dying. I had survived so long on calorie deficits and high-intensity workouts that full meals and rest days felt uncomfortable—painful, even. I'd gotten so used to the chains I wore, even as they dug into my flesh. Feeling them around my wrists reassured me that if I had nothing else, I was at least doing everything I could to stay small. During that time of recovery, what was most difficult was learning to let people in again. My chains made me feel safe, and I was still self-conscious about others seeing them. I had to hide to ensure they stayed concealed. That usually meant avoiding social situations where food was involved or pretending to eat (if absolutely necessary) to keep others from asking questions. Occasionally, I full-on lied. On one Santa Barbara afternoon, I got coffee with a friend. She suddenly got quiet, then looked me right in the eyes and said, "I feel like you're working out too much. And I never see you eat anything but scrambled eggs. You just seem different. Are you okay?"

When someone first meets me, they discover I turn bright red when I get embarrassed or put on the spot. My flushed face surely betrayed me, but I was simply uninterested in answering more questions or pretending I wanted to get better.

"Oh my gosh, yes!" I said. "We just don't see each other as much this semester. I'm training for that half-marathon, and I have just been trying to save money on food. You're sweet to ask, but I am so fine." She knew I was lying, but she dropped it. When I told her the truth many months later, I had to apologize for the dishonesty. She told me how much my secrecy had hurt her and damaged our friendship. We remained close, but I'm not sure our friendship ever fully recovered from my choice to hide my chains for months instead of prioritizing the health of our friendship.

My chains were finally broken off, but returning to freedom was hardly a clean process. I was on the road back to health, but the wounds left on my wrists were still open and festering.

No one knows that experience better than the Israelites. Adjusting to their newfound freedom proves just as difficult as escaping captivity. We find this small nation of nomads walking through the desert post-liberation, following a cloud by day and a pillar of fire by night (Exodus 13:21), with nothing to boast of but a promise that God will give them a land of their own. God sustains them with mysterious manna that can't be stored up and water from rocks in the dry, sparse desert. The Israelites go straight from the predictability of slavery to total dependence on a God they can't see. Then God gives them another covenant at Mount Sinai to build on the one He made with Abraham. In this covenant, God promises to bless and prosper Israel on the condition that they live according to His precepts and laws.

God's relationship to Israel would never change (per the Abrahamic covenant), but their flourishing was directly related to their obedience (per the Mosaic covenant). To rephrase, God will never give up on those He draws to Himself—never. But when we rebel against His ways, we may find ourselves struggling in a mess of our own.

That is precisely what happens to the nation of Israel. They rebel. Before Moses is even off the mountain at Sinai, Israel creates a golden calf to worship. Exodus 32 says a plague strikes the people as a punishment for this idolatry. No matter how many times God miraculously saves or provides, we see Israel scorning Him and running toward idols over and over.

Israel doesn't just fail to keep her end of the bargain; Israel blows her end of the bargain to shreds, leaving ash and dust. And every time, God bears the entire covenant by Himself, remaining committed to Israel and her flourishing because He tied Himself to His people in steadfast love (Hosea 11:4). However, He brings about her flourishing by disciplining Israel, which is thus just as much an act of love and pursuit as His acts of deliverance.

The life of David, Israel's greatest king, offers a meaningful microcosm of this relationship. Through the prophet Samuel, God seeks out David, a young shepherd boy in the fields. David—overlooked by his own father, who doesn't see him as worthy of being presented to Samuel along with his brothers—is the one God came to get. God sees beyond the external and into David's heart, and He knows David possesses the integrity and bravery of a king. From there, it is all up and to the right, and they all live happily ever after, right? *Psych.* David later commits one of the most serious, far-reaching sins recorded in the Bible, a sin of cowardice that manifests as lust, adultery, and murder.

Even in this catastrophic, disqualifying failure, God again seeks out David, this time through the prophet Nathan. Nathan does not come to play games; he comes to convict David of his wrongs and call him to swift repentance. God's discipline of David *is* the pursuit, and it is ultimately a key feature of David's story. And he knows it. "Surely your goodness and love will follow me all the days of my life," David writes in Psalm 23, "and I will dwell in the house of the Lord forever."

Do you see? God's pursuit of His people is not a new idea that starts in the New Testament when Jesus shows up. Rather, it's a central theme of the entire Bible from the very beginning. I skipped over a lot and I'm only getting started! I didn't even touch on Ruth, Esther, the Psalms, the Song of Solomon, or most of the prophets God sends to Israel to specifically tell His people that He wants them back—He's coming to get them. I skipped over many times and ways God pursues His people's hearts through provision, protection, and miracles. More than just a central theme of Scripture, God's pursuit of His beloved is a central aspect of who God is and how He feels *about you.*

Just trust me, at least for now. But also take time to read the whole Bible through the lens of God's pursuit. When you do, you will see this theme drawn out on nearly every page.

Fast-forward about fourteen generations straight from the line of David. You'll see God Himself in the flesh, again opting to bind Himself to the weakness of humanity (more literally than ever) for the sake of His people. Jesus Christ left the throne of heaven to save us from the power of sin and death. Jesus's coming to earth was the most fervent and determined vision of pursuit the world will ever know.

Whereas humans go after the things and people we think will offer some benefit or social advantage, Jesus extended Himself to humans who could offer Him nothing at all. More than that, He became sin on our behalf (2 Corinthians 5:21). Jesus in pursuit didn't just run after us. He went so far as to shoulder the consequences of our failure. Here's what I need you to see: Jesus Christ is the perfect God-intended picture of healthy pursuit.

We have all become so accustomed to a version of pursuit that is flippant, selfish, lustful, possessive, and weak that I think we fail to truly grasp the spectacular beauty in God's pursuit of humanity throughout Scripture. Pure, godly, sacrificial love necessarily involves pursuit. The love of God for His creation cannot remain at a distance; it must move *toward* and fight *on behalf of* us.

First Corinthians 13:4–7 (emphasis added) is a helpful framework for understanding what healthy pursuit looks like: "Love is patient, love is kind. It does not envy, it does not boast, it is not proud. *It does not dishonor others, it is not self-seeking, it is not easily angered, it keeps no record of wrongs.* Love does not delight in evil but rejoices with the truth. *It always protects, always trusts, always hopes, always perseveres.*"

If you have been the object of an unhealthy pursuit and were harmed by it, as my college classmate was, please hear this: God's pursuit is not self-seeking, nor is He easily angered. He will always protect you, always trust for you, always hope with you, and always persevere on your behalf. His goodness certainly follows us all the days of our lives.

Pursuit, as God intended and modeled, is love moved to its feet.

CHAPTER 2

FOR HIS NAME'S SAKE

"Now boarding Southwest flight 1440 to Phoenix Sky Harbor. If you are going to Phoenix today, please make your way to gate C47 at this time," the chipper disembodied voice announced through the terminal. That was our flight. My husband and I were on our way to Maui with our three-year-old son, Judah, and our one-year-old daughter, Thea. As we embarked on our journey, I was most worried about how Thea would react to the travel day and the possibility of missing her nap. I should have been worried about Judah. Unaware of the insanity before me on this fourteen-hour travel day, I was still blissfully naive and didn't realize that three-year-olds are feral animals. Sure, they warn you about the terrible twos, but not enough people discuss the *significantly* worse (at least in our experience) "threenager" phase.

My naivete wore off quickly, however, when Judah started running toward the boarding gate of the nearest plane. This would have been very helpful if it had been *our* boarding gate for *our* plane. It was not. Judah was running full steam ahead toward the gate for a plane headed to San Francisco (I guess a metropolitan destination sounded better that morning than the beach vacation we'd been planning for months). This flight was also in the boarding process, and Judah, ready to go, ran right to the gate agent.

At this point, I caught up with him and took hold of his little hand. "Judah, this isn't our plane!" I told him. "We have to keep walking a little farther."

The threenager, now emerging in full force, begged to differ. "I want to get on *this* plane!" he said firmly, ripping his hand from mine. I detected an edge in his voice that indicated the impending tantrum. But we had to move out of the San Francisco passengers' way, and more importantly, we had to get to our gate. I took a deep breath and squared up. "I know, sweet boy, but we have our very own plane, and we need to go right now so it doesn't leave without us." I grabbed his hand again, a little harder this time, and guided him in the direction we needed to go. This was the wrong move.

"I want to go on this plane! Let go of me! Let go of me! Let go of me!" Judah screamed at the top of his lungs, his voice echoing through the expansive terminal. By now, he was hitting, scratching, and biting my hand—anything to loosen my grip.

I tried to stay calm, even though I was tense and beginning to sweat. "Judah, you need to stay with Mama. I have to keep you close to me so I can keep you safe. I cannot let go of you until we are all on the right plane. All together."

Judah continued his tantrum, and "*Let go of me right now, Mama!*" elicited stares as we marched through the airport. Of course I wasn't going to let go. I wasn't about to allow my toddler to run onto a different plane than the one I was about to board. I am his mother, and in these early years of his life, my number one job is to keep him safe. When I gave birth to this child (whom I love deeply, despite the tantrum I now recount), the title of *mother*—and all that comes with it—became a permanent fixture of my identity. The safety and flourishing of my children will forever be one of my most fundamental priorities. Because of this identity shift, I could not let go of his angry little hand. I would not let go, because I would rather miss a trip to Hawaii than leave my son alone in an airport. *I will never let go*, because as his mom, I will always desire to be close to him and keep him safe.

Lest you assume this means I am going to be the crazy mother-in-law who never cuts the proverbial apron strings, I fully recognize that my ultimate goal for my kids is healthy independence from me. One day (sometime after he learns to read and tie his own shoes, I'm guessing), I will need to loosen my grip.

In becoming a mom, I began to see God's dedication to His children through fresh eyes and a new perspective. Like me when I had an iron grip around Judah's hand to ensure he stayed near me, God never lets go of us. While my relationship with my son will evolve over the next twenty years as he grows up, God's fierce dedication to being close to us never changes.

Like me in the airport that day when I was unwilling to depart from my child, God will never let go. And it's important to understand why God will never—can never—give up on us. What reason does God have to seek the lost sheep, especially when the sheep appear to be a dime a dozen and intent on running away? If I were a shepherd, there would come a time when I would let those ungrateful sheep go. But God doesn't seem to be willing to do that. *Why?*

GOD PURSUES US BECAUSE OF WHO WE ARE

My friend, I think it has *everything* to do with us.

Not because we are the main characters, and not because we are just so amazing that God has no choice but to run after us. Rather, it's about the core of our identity in light of God's own. As we touched on in the previous chapter, the creation of human beings was not the result of God's need but rather the overflow of the relationship thriving within the Trinity. Creation has always been for His name's sake.

> Remember, the essential nature of God is love—not stingy love, but generous love like a fountain splashing out joyfully. This bountiful God's gladness is enriched by having His Son at His side. He created that His love would be teeming, that it might be shared with His created image bearers, so that His Son might be the firstborn among

many. Creation is the beginning of a spreading, an outward explosion of love.[1]

In the Trinity, we also find the very essence of intimacy. Total oneness. Essential closeness and alignment. "Let us make mankind in our image," God says in Genesis 1:26. In the overflow of the Trinity, in the fullness of God's love that is the basis for His creation of humans, we also see that He created humans with the inherent identity of being His image bearers. The *imago Dei* in you is the form God chose to fashion using the overflow of His love. Thus, the way He relates to us is fundamental to our identities.

Quick theology check: Bearing the image of God is a far cry from *being* God or being divine in nature. Since God has chosen to fashion us to bear only a portion of His likeness, we are also fundamentally "other" from Him. God has all the power, all the time. Perhaps God is most unlike human beings, hateful and cruel as we know our species can be, in that God is the very essence of pure love.

That pure love compelled Him to breathe holy, perfect breath into the dust of creation; that pure love dignified dirt and marked it with a royal signet to claim it as His own and display His utter delight in what He had made.

Although the dust of the earth was formed into something spectacular (you!), the dust can never be the Creator. Yet in Him "we live and move and have our being" (Acts 17:28). In His perfect wisdom, He decided that the human image would uniquely and unequivocally resemble His own. God chose to tie His own image to ours.

GOD PURSUES US BECAUSE OF WHO HE IS

God seeks to draw us as His image bearers into the same perfect love and intimacy as within the Trinity. With this intimacy, we see God's pursuit fully realized. Of course, with perfection, pursuit is unnecessary. When human beings bear God's image, however, God does not do anything but continuously pursue us. Because God cannot be unfaithful to Himself, He cannot give up on the part of Himself that He chose for us to bear.

God comes after us with unconditional love and righteous jealousy whenever we embrace any identity other than what He has ordained for us: to be His image bearers. In the book of Hosea, God calls the prophet to marry a woman he knows will be unfaithful and to build a life with her. While we don't have much information on his wife, Gomer, we do know that she does not honor her marriage covenant with Hosea, and their relationship brutally illustrates how God felt watching Israel chase after false gods.

This prophetic picture, lived out in Hosea's own pain, extends into the lives of their children. God doesn't just call the prophet to be a living picture of Israel's spiritual reality; Hosea and Gomer's kids all receive names that speak to Israel's unfaithfulness to the covenant. These poor children, products of a sad, broken marriage, are named and identified by the sin and idols of their mother.

When Hosea's firstborn son is born, God says to Hosea, "Call him Jezreel, because I will soon punish the house of Jehu for the massacre at Jezreel, and I will put an end to the kingdom of Israel. In that day I will break Israel's bow in the Valley of Jezreel" (Hosea 1:4–5).

In Hebrew, Jezreel means "God sows." Based on this passage, God seems to sow judgment for the blood shed by Israel (represented by Jehu, whom we learn more about in 2 Kings 9–10). When that judgment is sown, the military power of Israel, represented by a bow, will break. The Hebrew word for "to sow" also translates as "to scatter." Jezreel's name points to the inescapable reality that judgment is coming for Israel; there is simply no other way around it. As the people of Israel trust in other nations for safety instead of trusting the God who has delivered them over and over, God must mercifully remind them how helpless they really are when they choose lesser gods. So judgment is coming, and Hosea's first son will live out his days bearing this truth for Israel to see.

Then Hosea and Gomer have a daughter, Lo-Ruhamah. And Jezreel's sister bears a truth as well:

> Gomer conceived again and gave birth to a daughter. Then the LORD said to Hosea, "Call her Lo-Ruhamah (which means "not loved"), for I will no longer show love to Israel, that I should at all forgive them. Yet I will show love to Judah; and I will save them—not by bow, sword or battle, or by horses and horsemen, but I, the LORD their God, will save them." (Hosea 1:6–7)

This tells me that God again graciously gives Israel time to process the prophetic message of Hosea and his family and to repent. As 2 Peter 3:9 says, "The Lord is not slow in keeping his promise, as some understand slowness. Instead, he is patient with you, not wanting anyone to perish, but everyone to come to repentance."

Israel has already heard that a reckoning is coming. Now God underlines the urgency of the situation: The love you take for granted will depart if you do not repent. Poor baby girl Lo-Ruhamah will be known forever by the departure of God's love, mercy, and forgiveness for His people. Remember when God spoke to Moses in Exodus 34:6–7 (NRSV)?

> "The Lord, the Lord,
> a God merciful and gracious,
> slow to anger,
> and abounding in steadfast love and faithfulness,
> keeping steadfast love for the thousandth
> generation,
> forgiving iniquity and transgression and sin,
> yet by no means clearing the guilty,
> but visiting the iniquity of the parents
> upon the children
> and the children's children
> to the third and the fourth generation."

This passage is so well known because it forms one of the key pieces of Israel's covenantal relationship with God and gives us a clear picture of how God relates to Israel. Lo-Ruhamah's name does not just represent judgment; her name is a jarring reversal of and challenge to how Israel understands itself. But it still isn't enough to shake God's people out of their rebellion.

> After she had weaned Lo-Ruhamah, Gomer had another son. Then the Lord said, "Call him Lo-Ammi (which means "not my people"), for you are not my people, and I am not your God." (Hosea 1:8–9)

With the birth of this new child, God tries to shake the people awake by pressing on the deepest part of the Israelite identity: You are not acting like My people, so how am I supposed to be your God?

In Exodus 6:7, God makes a promise to Moses: "I will take you as my own people, and I will be your God. Then you will know that I am the Lord your God, who brought you out from under the yoke of the Egyptians." God makes a similar promise to Abraham in Genesis 17:7. This relationship between God and Israel is not just part of Israel's identity; it is the entirety of Israel's identity (Deuteronomy 7:7–9). Lo-Ammi bears the heavy burden of informing Israel with his very identity that Israel has failed in its covenant with God and thus will be alone.

The sin of Israel is responsible for the names of these children and the judgment they represent. Israel's idolatry determines these kids' identities, just as the Israelites' idolatry completely absorbs their own identity. I have seen the exact same effect of sin and idolatry in my own life: The eating disorder I struggled with in college took over all my priorities and interests. My love for God was no longer as central to my identity as my desire to be thin. Have you experienced how sin can rob you of your true identity and hollow you out?

When you take a step back and look at what sin does to your life and your heart, you see a black hole: just a big, dark, all-consuming nothingness where there used to be vibrancy and joy. Sin doesn't let you keep anything of your real identity—who God created you to be—because sin has to have it all.

What we've read up to this point in Hosea is enough to leave us hopeless. God's warnings should have been enough to make Israel turn around and run back to God. But this is what makes the book of Hosea so starkly beautiful (and tough to interpret in some parts): God pronounces judgment in dark, scary ways and then almost immediately follows that judgment with a bright, beautiful assurance of hope:

> "Yet the Israelites will be like the sand on the seashore, which cannot be measured or counted. In the place where it was said to them, 'You are not my people,' they will be called 'children of the living God.' The people of Judah and the people of Israel will come together; they will appoint one leader and will come up out of the land, for great will be the day of Jezreel. . . .
>
> *"Say of your brothers, 'My people,' and of your sisters, 'My loved one.'"* (Hosea 1:10–11; 2:1, emphasis added)

Whereas God's judgment will scatter Israel ("Jezreel"), God has already promised—before the judgment even occurs—that His people will nonetheless thrive and grow. He restates His famous promise to Abraham (Genesis 22:17–18), Israel's unfaithfulness apparently notwithstanding. In the beginning of this passage, Jezreel represents violence and death; in this last verse of the chapter, Jezreel depicts a place of unity and flourishing.

Lo-Ruhamah, the little girl who was "not loved" and had to wear that name wherever she went, is now called His loved one. But she is not just one among many. She will be known as *His* loved one, the beloved of the God of Israel. Her life, then, speaks to God's unquenchable love for His people Israel.

And although God just said Israel would no longer be His people ("Lo-Ammi"), He has ordained to make them His again with no mention of their side of the bargain. They are not just God's people but children of the living God; no amount of failure can alter their status before God. God extends Himself well beyond the bounds of the original Old Testament covenants to carry the full burden of Israel's unfaithfulness. Lo-Ammi will not be forgotten after all, and God resolves again to make the Israelites children of the living God (Hosea 1:10). Israel is God's people by His mercy alone.

While the judgment will still come, as a loving Father disciplines His children, Hosea shows right off the bat that God has not given up on His beloved. He is a good father forever committed to the flourishing of His kids. Whereas we *thought* God's character depended on our behavior, His mercy and steadfast love are inextricable from the way He relates to us:

> But Zion said, "The Lord has forsaken me;
> my Lord has forgotten me."
> Can a woman forget her nursing child

or show no compassion for the child of her womb?
Even these might forget,
yet I will not forget you.
See, I have inscribed you on the palms of my hands;
your walls are continually before me.
(Isaiah 49:14–16 NRSV)

Throughout the Old Testament, we see God's loyal, unfailing love for His people referred to as the Hebrew word *khesed.* You may have seen *khesed* translated as "steadfast love" or "lovingkindness." *Khesed* is love that doesn't give up, and it's love that is determined to stay faithful even when the recipient of that love strays.

I recently made a new friend who is a few years ahead of me in life. She found out that her husband, previously a pastor, had a monthslong affair with a sex worker in a different state. Coincident with this betrayal, he walked away from his lifelong faith. As the wife of a pastor, I know that both events would absolutely gut me. If I'm totally honest, either one could send me into my own crisis of faith. As my friend revealed more details about what she had experienced the past few years, I was nearly brought to tears when I imagined the pain she had walked through. But I was mostly struck by her belief in and dedication to her husband's restoration. Her retelling of the events was peppered with grace.

"He's truly an amazing dad, so this has been really hard on our kids," she told me.

"Ever since I found out, he's been so committed to making things right, and I really appreciate that," she said.

"He says his faith was all an act, but it's not true. I was there," she said with confidence as she expressed her commitment to reminding him of all God had done in his life.

At one point I said to her, "I don't know how you're able to show so much grace. I'm not sure I would have it in me."

Her response stuck in my mind and has stayed ever since: "You know, for the past two years I have been praying that God would reveal Himself to my husband. And God has showed me that He is using me to do just that."

That very week, her husband returned to church with their family for the first time in a long time. This kind of covenantal love—the kind that holds on and won't let go—is *khesed* love. My friend's commitment to both the healing of her broken marriage and the renewed faith of an unfaithful spouse is a beautiful picture of God's unconditional love for us.

(Quick disclaimer: While I find my friend's response to her husband's infidelity redemptive and powerful, I am all too aware that many people have lived through similar circumstances with very different endings. For many of these stories, I am confident that divorce was likely the only option, as the unfaithful party effectively chose to walk away from the marriage covenant. Yes, we should seek to model God's faithfulness, and we should fight hard for our marriages, even when they are broken. But this story is not meant to imply that you are unfaithful and weak if you were forced to end a marriage because of an unfaithful spouse.)

When we trace the Old Testament story from the beginning, we see that God's intention is to bless the world by using Israel as a conduit for Jesus Christ, who then rights all the wrongs of

Adam and Eve's sin for all nations, tribes, peoples, and tongues (Revelation 7:9). To achieve this, His covenant cannot rest on the moral dependability of human beings.

The covenant was never contingent on human perfection, because it was always grounded in the *khesed* love that emanates from God's self, the Trinity. As long as God's image bearers are far from Him, God will pursue them. He will always seek that perfect intimacy with those who bear Godlikeness. Until He returns to gather all creation to Himself and finally right all the wrongs and mend all the brokenness, He will draw us toward Himself.

God is faithful in His love toward us because God is faithful to Himself. He cannot deny His own nature, and He is love. That divine love doesn't falter. The love He breathed into you cannot deny its own steadfastness. This truth should awaken a sense of awe and a desire to give Him glory. Why? When we focus on who God is and what He has done for us, we acknowledge God in His proper place: "The one who comes from above is above all; the one who is from the earth belongs to the earth, and speaks as one from the earth. The one who comes from heaven is above all" (John 3:31). It's not about us. It's about Christ in us. When we see the beauty in knowing our purpose in life is all about Him, we can get out of the way and give Him the glory and honor He deserves. We find an earnest, reciprocal love for this God—the One who is always faithful—rising in our hearts.

Let's take a moment to recap:

1. *God didn't create you for your glory but for His.*

   That means God put something in you that is capable

of holiness and beauty. You were created to glorify the God of the universe, which is much more wonderful than spending your days trying to make your own name great. See it as the honor it is.

2. *God doesn't need you.*

   He is wholly sufficient in Himself, in the joy and intimacy of the Trinity.

   No, friend, God *wanted* you. And not just that—God knit your story into His grand plan for the salvation of the world. He wants you to participate in what He is doing. Singer Bono once said, "Stop asking God to bless what you're doing. Find out what God is doing, 'cause it's already blessed."[2]

3. *God doesn't pursue you because you are worthy but because He is.*

   The image of God on you and in you calls you to intimacy with Him and necessitates that He pursue you until that perfect intimacy is realized. You don't need to spend one more moment trying to be good enough, because the image of God is enough to make you worthy. God does not give up on you, because *khesed* love is who He is.

Martin Luther summed up these ideas this way: "The love of God does not find, but creates, that which is pleasing to it. . . . Rather than seeking its own good, the love of God flows forth and bestows good. Therefore sinners are attractive because they are loved; they are not loved because they are attractive."[3]

There's something freeing and lovely about that truth: God

said we are worth dying for, and then He did die for us, so we simply *are.* When God assigns value and dignity, something simply *is.* Because of His *khesed* love, God desires to be with us and near us. Look at what He has to say in Isaiah 43:4–7:

> "Since you are precious and honored in my sight,
> and because I love you,
> I will give people in exchange for you,
> nations in exchange for your life.
> Do not be afraid, for I am with you;
> I will bring your children from the east
> and gather you from the west.
> I will say to the north, 'Give them up!'
> and to the south, 'Do not hold them back.'
> Bring my sons from afar
> and my daughters from the ends of the earth—
> everyone who is called by my name,
> whom I created for my glory,
> whom I formed and made."

God bound Himself to you by His own will and for His glory. God won't abandon you. God has determined that you are forever the object of His pursuit. It's for His name's sake. Rest in His *khesed* love.

CHAPTER 3

THE LION THAT SAVES

"I was praying you'd get caught."

Those words were terrifying at the time, but they had a massive impact on how I came to understand the ways God pursues us. But I need to tell you the story first.

I was sixteen years old and standing in a bagel shop near my high school with my friend. It was 2008, and I was holding my brand-new, very cool smartphone (not to brag, but it was an LG enV2—cutting-edge technology at the time). I was telling my friend about the night before, when my mom almost found out that I had recently started partying with my friends.

You see, my mom had a rule about my cell phone: I had to turn it in every night at nine. At that point, any calls had to go through the landline. That night, since it was after nine, I was on the landline in my basement, cooking up a plan for the coming weekend with my friend Rachel. "You need to tell your mom that you're sleeping here, and I will tell my mom we're sleeping at your house," I said. "Then we can walk up to the McDonald's where the guys can pick us up, and we can both sleep at Destiny's house!" I summarized the plan with her to make sure we were on the same page. My mom wasn't the type to listen in on my calls, so I wasn't worried.

Before I hung up the phone, I heard: *Click.*

My hands went clammy, and I felt my face getting hot. *Oh no, oh no, oh no.*

"Rachel, I've got to go. I think my mom heard that," I said.

I made my way upstairs, not sure how I was going to play this. My mom looked angry when I found her in her room.

Should I own up to my plans? Should I tell her the truth? I wondered. Then I shrugged it off. Of course not. Something to know about me is that I am going to double down every time.

So I said, "Mom, Rachel and I have this inside joke, and it gets crazy and out of hand sometimes. We like to make fun of the kids who are partying all the time, so we like pretending to be them and saying all the dumb things they say. It's funny to us, but I can see how it would seem bad! I am really sorry, and we don't have any plans to do anything. Destiny isn't even in town this weekend."

After a long conversation and a lot of skepticism, my mother gave up on grilling me. What else could she do? I hadn't done anything, other than premeditating my devious plans. I went to school the next morning feeling relieved, sly, and satisfied with how I manipulated her.

When I went to the bagel shop for lunch with my friend and I recounted everything from the night before, I said to her, "I just said whatever I had to, to get out of it, and it worked."

And then an act of God. I looked down at my cell phone and saw that a phone call had started thirty seconds earlier. *Huh?* I looked closer. It was my mom. I held the phone to my ear, trying to act natural. "Oh, hi, Mom! Did you call me?" My voice was shaky and high-pitched, with every ounce of my smugness evaporating on the spot.

Now she was the smug one. "I heard everything," she said. "We're going to talk when you get home. When the phone rang just seconds ago, I was right in the middle of praying to the Lord that you would get caught. What do you know?"

My blood ran cold. My mind raced. I was done for. I went home that day to face a nice long chat about underage drinking and lying to my parents. I also found myself grounded from leaving the house and from using a cell phone for the next two months. While I was upset at the punishment, I also remember understanding where my mom was coming from. I was clearly in the wrong.

To figuratively put my hand on the Bible—and this detail stuck with me—just days before, I had reprogrammed my speed dials, and I hadn't re-added my home phone number yet. There was no way I could have accidentally dialed all ten digits that led to calling my mom. I was scared, sure, but I was also certain I had been on the business end of a genuine act of God. He had shown up in my life and pursued me. This time, His pursuit looked like intervening in my sin and disciplining me when I was wandering. During those next few months of being homebound, I began to read my Bible again and found a renewed faith. During that season of discipline, I also became convinced I wanted to dedicate my life to serving Jesus.

As I learned from that experience, God pursues us not only through *khesed* love but also through His discipline. The word *discipline* is scary to us if we have individualistic sensibilities. For many of us, discipline evokes memories of being grounded or spanked by our parents when we were little kids. In extreme situations, perhaps abusive actions were falsely labeled as "discipline" as an attempt to justify and excuse them. Whatever the case may be, discipline is not a word we typically associate with the warm fuzzies. I want to reframe our understanding of the word, not because it's easy when God thwarts our plans or interferes with our sin, but because administering good discipline is one of the most loving things a good Father can do.

For example, discipline accomplishes the following for your children when performed calmly and consistently:

- protects your child from danger
- helps your child learn self-control and self-discipline
- helps your child develop a sense of responsibility
- instills values[1]

As the mother of a three-year-old boy, I feel particularly qualified to speak on disciplining a child. Right now, my son's prefrontal cortex—the part of his brain responsible for many processes related to impulse control, decision-making, and rule following—is basically just a cute little glob of Silly Putty. Over the next few years, this part of his brain will develop rapidly, but for now, I am his prefrontal cortex. I am the one who makes sure he does not acquiesce to every intrusive thought that comes through his brain (such as the problematic, albeit creative, idea to dip his sister's face in ranch dressing at dinner). I am the one who makes the decisions he can't and walks him through decisions his brain is ready for (such as choosing between the Lightning McQueen or the monster truck underwear). I am the one who sets the rules that he gets to learn how to follow so that we can set him up for success in our society down the road and hope he doesn't break a law that could land him in prison.

I have a newfound appreciation for this aspect of God as Father. Through the guiding Holy Spirit, He forms us into the people He created us to be. He knows our limitations and our immaturity, and He walks with us as we grow in wisdom. Discipline is an essential piece of the puzzle.

Just like my young son, we are sometimes simply too ignorant and limited in our perspective to make good choices. We may act like little sheep, hung up on a really good patch of grass. We exclaim, "Ooh, a thistle!" and we wander from the rest of the flock. Then we follow a bumblebee through the meadow, and we walk alongside the riverbank looking at rocks. Soon we're so far from the flock that we're in danger; we're now a target for predators, and if we get injured, we will be stuck. Our lack of self-control, even when it's innocent, leads us to destruction.

As the parable of the good shepherd so clearly shows (see Matthew 18:12–14), God refuses to lose us because of our own ignorance. He is the Good Shepherd going out to find that one sheep and leaving the other ninety-nine behind. And then He must teach us to remain in His pasture, lest we find ourselves alone and in danger.

When God interrupts our plans, we're likely to get frustrated. We feel offended by the implication that we are veering off course or acting in ignorance. Rescue often feels like an attack. Boundaries meant to protect us feel like cages. When God goes out and brings us back from these situations, rescue itself is a form of discipline. Good discipline isn't about harsh punishment. It's about redirecting us to safe, healthy spaces; it's about teaching us that staying close to Him is the best place to be.

Because He is a good Father and the Good Shepherd, God pursues us when we wander, willfully or ignorantly, so He can save us from our futile plans (at best) and our rebellion (at worst). I think God routinely and gently corrects us in those slipups and sins we commit in ignorance. This correction is a natural part of our spiritual formation when we have the Holy Spirit within us. Sometimes, though, we do more than just make ignorant mistakes. Sometimes we intentionally rebel against the Shepherd.

I can speak to what rebelling against the Shepherd is like. Although my eating disorder was a disease on one level, I was also cognizant as I made choices that idolized my physical body. I opted for taking a morning run instead of reading my Bible, because I had to fit in a workout to make sure I was losing weight. I chose not to get lunch with friends who cared about me, because it was too difficult to count the calories and I preferred the control of eating the small portions I consumed when I ate by myself. I made little choices that did not honor God's design for me well before the disease fully took away my sense of agency. My choice to make an idol out of my thinness pushed me out of the driver's seat. And although I don't think this progression necessarily applies to all people who struggle with eating disorders, what I am describing is true of my experience at the early stages of this disease.

The truth is, while we are choosing to rebel—to go after idols instead of receiving the love God freely offers us—the time may come when God simply won't stand for it anymore. His discipline can feel swift and harsh, like it's stopping us in our tracks. Sometimes His discipline looks like us watching everything in our lives fall apart as God tries to show us how futile our rebellion is. Because of His love for us, God acts radically and decisively to save us from ourselves. The results can feel as loud and terrifying as a roaring lion.

When my toddler threw a tantrum after I made him get off the swing, he ran full steam ahead into the street. Let me tell you: I didn't call out sweetly to him. I didn't patiently redirect his steps. I sprinted into the road, swept him up, and marched that little boy right into our house.

In my case, God disrupted my rebellion by allowing me to see the impact of my idolatry. He allowed me to experience the fallout from my decisions and to feel the consequences of my actions. I sacrificed relationships, integrity, and health on the altar of thinness. I chose workouts over sleep, and I chose sitting at home with small portions of low-calorie foods over enjoying celebrations with people I loved. I became good at lying about my problem and, in the process, became more comfortable with lying in general. Instead of insulating me from these consequences, God allowed me to sit with them for a while. My body didn't feel good because I was malnourished and vitamin deficient. I felt the aches in my bones and the fatigue in my muscles. I saw my dry skin and my thinning hair. Many friendships had deteriorated in the previous months, and I was forced to feel just how profoundly I had isolated myself. Listening to the call to prayer in the dark early morning hours in my Istanbul Airbnb, I was more aware than ever of how far off course I had gotten, and how empty and sad my eating disorder had left me.

When I read Hosea 5:13–14 in that apartment, I felt the weight of not being rescued (at least not in the instantaneous way I would have preferred): "When Ephraim saw his sickness, and Judah his sores, then Ephraim turned to Assyria, and sent to the great king for help. But he is not able to cure you, not able to heal your sores. For I will be like a lion to Ephraim, like a great lion to Judah. I will tear them to pieces and go away; I will carry them off, with no one to rescue them."

Ephraim and Judah represent the people of Israel, who were split into two kingdoms during this time. God says here that He allowed these two unfaithful peoples to experience the effects of the sickness they had visited on themselves, just as I was experiencing the full weight of the sickness I had visited on myself.

When we attach our hope to an idol and find our joy in something false, we believe we will find sustenance there. For someone to pry our hands free and take us to the water of truth feels offensive. It might even feel like a death sentence. The young

Lion that tears apart Ephraim and Judah and carries them off into the wilderness—that Lion may seem like a predator. When God forcibly extracts us from our rebellion, we often view Him this way, particularly when we still believe that we might find an alternate source of life and abundance within our sin. Truly, we will die if we persist in this delusion. If we insist on seeking our sustenance from a source that cannot truly nourish us, we will spiritually waste away. To save us, God must tear us away from whatever false idol we have hitched our hope to.

I read past devastating chapters 6–10 in Hosea to see what this Lion does in chapter 11, verses 8 and 10–11:

> "How can I give you up, Ephraim?
>   How can I hand you over, Israel?
> How can I treat you like Admah?
>   How can I make you like Zeboyim?
> My heart is changed within me;
>   all my compassion is aroused. . . .
> They will follow the LORD;
>   he will roar like a lion.
> When he roars,
>   his children will come trembling from
>   the west.
> They will come from Egypt,
>   trembling like sparrows,
>   from Assyria, fluttering like doves.
> I will settle them in their homes,"
>   declares the LORD.

Here we find beautiful news. This same Lion not only wants to allure us, leading us into the wilderness and speaking tenderly to us (Hosea 2:14), but now His compassion is aroused.

This fierce Lion is here to tear us away, yes, but not to kill. The Lion draws us into the desert, where He speaks tenderly and where He restores. What feels like death becomes the sweetest restoration of life and transforms us into who God has always wanted us to be. It reminds me of a powerful dialogue C. S. Lewis wrote in *The Lion, the Witch and the Wardrobe*:

> "Aslan is a lion—*the* Lion, the great Lion."
>
> "Ooh!" said Susan, "I'd thought he was a man. Is he—quite safe? I shall feel rather nervous about meeting a lion." . . .
>
> "Safe?" said Mr. Beaver. . . . "Who said anything about safe? 'Course he isn't safe. But he's good. He's the King, I tell you."[2]

I am both afraid and relieved to know that there is a God who will seek me out and forcibly extract the evil that wants me dead—even the evil I invite in, whether purposefully or in ignorance.

Being close to this good and holy God means the sin has to die. And when your identity is intertwined with that sin, its death will hurt. It may feel excruciating. What our deluded, deceived minds thought was a bloodthirsty predator coming to kill us has been the Lion of Judah all along, coming to carry us to a quiet place. When God tears you away from the sin that's destroying you and carries you deep into the wilderness, it may look like a death sentence. But in the wilderness we can finally rest in His love and peace.

This reminds me of Jonah. If anyone ever rebelled against God and His purposes, it was him.

> The word of the LORD came to Jonah son of Amittai: "Go to the great city of Nineveh and preach against it, because its wickedness has come up before me."
>
> But Jonah ran away from the LORD and headed for Tarshish. (Jonah 1:1–3)

Jonah doesn't just disobey God, and he doesn't just head to the next town over. Jonah beelines for the nearest port city and boards a ship headed to Tarshish, 2,500 miles away via sea voyage and at least a three-week journey. This man is so determined to be uninvolved in God's specific plan for him that he decides to put Psalm 139:7 to the test: "Where can I go from your Spirit? Where can I flee from your presence?"

The answer, as the psalmist knew, is nowhere. And Jonah finds this out too. The boat is ravaged by storms threatening to tear it apart. The group determines that Jonah, who is fleeing from his God, needs to get right with his deity if they all are to survive. Jonah knows precisely what is going on and insists they throw him overboard. They don't want to—they try to find another way—but ultimately, they must.

And the seas calm instantly.

> Now the LORD provided a huge fish to swallow Jonah, and Jonah was in the belly of the fish three days and three nights. (Jonah 1:17)

See that? God ordains and equips Jonah for evangelism, and it is going to happen, even in his rebellion. God proves Himself true and superior to other gods, even in this mess. The men in that boat encounter truth through Jonah, even in these harrowing circumstances.

Additionally, the whale is God's provision; it saves Jonah from sure death. The terrifying vision of a gigantic whale closing its mouth over your body and the subsequent realization that you are still alive is the stuff of horror movies; nonetheless, being swallowed by the whale allows Jonah to survive. For someone like me with a slight and inexplicable fear of whales, this lands easily: Just like the young Lion that tears Gomer away from her false lovers and forcibly removes Israel from her idols, the mouth of the whale looks like death and brings true life.

God gives Jonah the opportunity to be obedient and responsive straightaway. Like so many of us, Jonah is so sure of his own insufficiency that it drives him to rebel and reject God's limitlessness. God graciously doesn't give up on him and find someone new. God refines Jonah in the storm he brought on himself. God reaches lost people despite and *because of* Jonah's failure, and He uses a traumatic event to restore Jonah to his rightful calling and, ultimately, his true identity as a prophet of God.

Within the belly of the whale, Jonah says this prayer, which demonstrates his dramatic, counterintuitive restoration:

> "Those who cling to worthless idols
> turn away from God's love for them.

But I, with shouts of grateful praise,
    will sacrifice to you.
What I have vowed I will make good.
    I will say, 'Salvation comes from the LORD.'"
        (Jonah 2:8–9)

God lets Jonah out of the whale, and Jonah goes to Nineveh. The people are shockingly receptive to the call to reform their ways. They grieve and mourn before God. They repent.

Our own stories of God's pursuit through our rebellion aren't linear. Your testimony doesn't end when you accept Christ. There will be ups and downs. You will fail God over and over. But that's the point: He continues to come after you, and He continues to draw you into circumstances that will form you into the person He made you to be. Rinse and repeat. Once you are His, that's the journey you begin.

All of this—the redirection when we wander, the forceful rescue missions when we rebel, the spiritual formation we experience in the pain that results from our own sin and in our liberation from it—is God's discipline of us, His beloved image bearers.

When God disciplines you, God pursues you. God leads you from destruction into goodness. To get a clear picture of God's pursuit, we need look no further than Psalm 23:

The LORD is my shepherd, I lack nothing.
    He makes me lie down in green pastures,
he leads me beside quiet waters,
    he refreshes my soul.

He guides me along the right paths
    for his name's sake.
Even though I walk
    through the darkest valley,
I will fear no evil,
    for you are with me;
your rod and your staff,
    they comfort me.

You prepare a table before me
    in the presence of my enemies.
You anoint my head with oil;
    my cup overflows.
Surely your goodness and love will follow me
    all the days of my life,
and I will dwell in the house of the LORD
    forever.

The Good Shepherd pursues us when we wander and leads us into peace. He makes us lie down (even when we would keep walking). His rod and His staff are instruments of comfort—as they prod and firmly direct, they offer protection and guidance.

God as our Shepherd leads as He follows. He is not only ahead, leading us without looking back, and He is not only behind, focusing exclusively on correction when we take the wrong step. No, the psalmist writes, "You go before me and follow me. You place your hand of blessing on my head" (Psalm 139:5 NLT). God's pursuit means we are completely covered on all sides.

Sometimes God leads as a massive and commanding pillar of fire or smoke in the distance. Sometimes He's the still, small voice beckoning us to listen closely. For me, His guidance came through the gentle nudges of the Good Shepherd's rod reminding me to stay the course. I've felt the uncomfortable crook of His staff around my neck and I've been offended by it, only to look over my shoulder and see the cliff He swept me away from just as my foot began to slip. The Good Shepherd, with His goodness and mercy, is always pursuing (i.e., *following*) the sheep to get them out of the valleys they've found themselves in and toward the green pastures He alone knows the way to.

Can we, like the psalmist, take comfort in the discipline of God?

Can we celebrate and be amazed by a God who wants to be involved in our healthy formation as a good engaged parent?

Can we, like Jonah, rejoice with shouts of praise that God is our salvation and, even in the brutal moments that feel unfair and unforgiving, remember that God's love is sometimes uncomfortable but always steadfast?

Surely goodness and mercy are pursuing us all the days of our lives.

CHAPTER 4

WHEN IT FEELS LIKE GOD HAS GIVEN UP

I was driving back to my college campus in Santa Barbara, California, after a short break I'd spent in Orange County, just a few hours south. For some reason, I was making the drive around 9:00 p.m., and I came across some night construction (a common occurrence in the greater LA area). I was subsequently routed on a detour through a part of the city I didn't know. Soon my phone died. I was lost, and my internal compass was rendered useless amid the endless concrete and tiny fluorescent signs for chain restaurants and convenience stores.

Naturally curious and open to exploring, I stayed calm and took in the new sights and sounds while I did my best to weave my way to the freeway. Soon, though, I realized my car needed gas. I pulled into the first gas station I saw. After parking, I got out and quickly swiped my credit card to start the pump. But my card wasn't working. I looked around and saw that people, including a group of men I hadn't noticed previously, were looking at me. I suddenly had a sadly familiar feeling in the pit of my stomach—I sensed I might not be safe, and I started to panic. In that moment, I was acutely aware that no one knew where I was. I hadn't bothered to tell any of my friends at school when I planned to be back. I hadn't talked to my parents that day, and this was well before the Find My Friends app showed you the GPS location of all your loved ones. My godmother, whom I had been staying with, knew I was somewhere between Orange County and Santa Barbara, but that meant absolutely nothing in one of the most populous and expansive areas in the country. I was utterly alone. I was afraid and stuck, and no one even knew to be worried about me.

The problem was easily resolved when I realized that this gas station didn't accept credit cards, so I headed to the next one. After fueling up there, I asked a kind-looking person for directions to the 101 and soon was on my way.

At that first gas station, I likely wasn't in grave danger. But the feeling of being alone and unknown, even for just a moment, stuck with me.

Have you ever felt that way with God? Like you're all alone, afraid and disoriented, and He's not looking for you?

In writing this book about God's relentless, steadfast pursuit, I am deeply aware of how many people have never felt like they have experienced it. With every line I write, I am reminded of tragic stories of people whom God didn't save or heal. What do we make of God's pursuit when we watch a formerly vibrant believer walk away from their faith and never look back? What does God's pursuit mean for that person in a hospital room with a terminal diagnosis? What does it mean for the mother whose son overdosed after she prayed for years that he would be liberated from addiction?

Many biblical texts offer fertile ground for debate on the subject. If you're like me and believe that (1) we only come to know God through His pursuit and that (2) God is indeed pursuing all humanity, these texts might require some wrestling with. I offer these to show that God's pursuit can look very different from what we imagine. Even in these moments when God appears to be far away, He is very near.

Here is just a handful of examples:

- Genesis 18–19: Here we get the full story of the destruction of Sodom and Gomorrah, two entire cities destroyed by God because of the inhabitants' wickedness. This story comes up again and again as proof for the skeptic that God isn't gracious at all, but rigid and violent and heavy-handed in His punishment of anyone who veers from His commandments. Will God destroy us if we rebel, instead of continuing to run after us? This example certainly doesn't look like pursuit.
- Romans 1:24–25 says, "Therefore God gave them over in the sinful desires of their hearts to sexual impurity

for the degrading of their bodies with one another. They exchanged the truth about God for a lie, and worshiped and served created things rather than the Creator—who is forever praised. Amen." Evidently, it's possible for us to lean into sin with such intention that God allows us to do so unrestrained. How can God pursue us if God gives us over to evil?

- Deuteronomy 28:15–68 is entitled "Curses for Disobedience" in the NIV translation. Here God explains the consequences of disobedience, most notably exile from the promised land. See verses 15–18: "However, if you do not obey the LORD your God and do not carefully follow all his commands and decrees I am giving you today, all these curses will come on you and overtake you: You will be cursed in the city and cursed in the country. Your basket and your kneading trough will be cursed. The fruit of your womb will be cursed, and the crops of your land, and the calves of your herds and the lambs of your flocks." If God visits such severe consequences on the Israelites because of their disobedience, is God's love conditional?

As someone deeply convinced of God's pursuit in the face of these hard truths, I need to tell you that these represent just a tiny sample of passages that could, without context, make you wonder if God's love is as steadfast as we are told, or if perhaps it is reserved only for a subset of chosen people. In this chapter, we're not shying away from those hard, valid questions. We're talking about them so that you will see another facet of God's pursuit.

From the start, it's important to understand that much of Scripture contains an inherent tension. How can God be all-knowing, all-powerful, and all-good? How can God be three persons and yet remain one? How can Jesus be both fully human and fully divine? As we engage in this discussion, we must remember that, as Glenn Packiam puts it, "A God you can explain is a God you can contain. And a God you can contain can't be worshipped."[1] God is so massive and powerful that He created solar systems. He's so precise and intentional that He designed your tiniest cells. And yet you—who are unable to fully comprehend all that—somehow expect to completely grasp how He does things? No. And you wouldn't want to. God is worthy of worship partly because His ways are so high above our own, and His vastness and specificity are so far beyond our own. If you ever find you can fully wrap your mind around the nature of a god, it's not something you should bow before.

So when we bump into these matters that confound us, we need not allow them to drive us straight into doubt (although if we end up there, God isn't afraid of that either). When we encounter a contradiction, or what seems like one, we should try to embrace the mystery of it all. Then we can rest in knowing that the ways of God will remain largely beyond our perception and comprehension. That doesn't mean you stop trying to understand; it means you approach complex, challenging ideas and thoughts with humility and a supernatural sense of peace.

I live in Colorado, where the air is dry, the sun burns hot, and the wind sweeping through mountain valleys can be powerful—ideal conditions for forest fires. Too many times, I have looked to the horizon and seen a plume of smoke, followed shortly by ash and the telltale campfire smell in the air. These fires wreak havoc on the natural landscape and the communities throughout it. Only a few years ago, in January 2022, the Marshall fire incinerated over one thousand homes in Boulder County, a short drive from where I live.

To prevent these fires and keep the natural environment healthy, forest rangers do what is called a *prescribed burn*, which is intentionally initiating and managing a forest fire within specific boundaries to keep the land healthy. According to the National Forest Service, "The right fire at the right place at the right time:

- Reduces hazardous fuels, protecting human communities from extreme fires;
- Minimizes the spread of pest insects and disease;
- Removes unwanted species that threaten species native to an ecosystem;
- Provides forage for game;
- Improves habitat for threatened and endangered species;
- Recycles nutrients back to the soil; and
- Promotes the growth of trees, wildflowers, and other plants."[2]

Environmental restoration and the best interests of the land sometimes require a controlled burn. The goal isn't to burn thriving live trees; the goal is to get rid of fallen branches, brush, and dead trees that threaten the well-being of the forest. Jesus alludes to something similar in John 15:5–6 (NRSV): "I am the vine;

you are the branches. Those who abide in me and I in them bear much fruit, because apart from me you can do nothing. Whoever does not abide in me is thrown away like a branch and withers; such branches are gathered, thrown into the fire, and burned."

When enough dry dead branches collect, is God not obligated—for the good and health of the greater ecosystem—to conduct a kind of controlled burn? I am reminded of the story of Noah and the flood, one of those accounts that will always be at the forefront of any debate about God's love and sovereignty. Why? Just look at this passage from Genesis 6:11–13:

> Now the earth was corrupt in God's sight and was full of violence. God saw how corrupt the earth had become, for all the people on earth had corrupted their ways. So God said to Noah, "I am going to put an end to all people, for the earth is filled with violence because of them. I am surely going to destroy both them and the earth."

Noah, patriarch of the final righteous family on the face of the earth, obeys God's commands and builds an ark for himself and his family. Ostensibly he explains to his neighbors why. And God does what He says. He floods the earth for 150 days, and everyone dies except for Noah, his family, and the animals God told Noah to fill the ark with.

When God decides that the entire population of the earth is too wicked to be redeemed and opts to obliterate them from existence, does that mean He has ceased to pursue them? It's a fair question. It was hard for me to reconcile that one.

But the answer is no. God's act of destruction remains an act of pursuit—toward Noah and his family, but more importantly toward the rest of humanity that comes after Noah.

What do we know about the objects of God's destruction here? Look at Genesis 6:5–6: "The Lord saw how great the wickedness of the human race had become on the earth, and that every inclination of the thoughts of the human heart was only evil all the time. The Lord regretted that he had made human beings."

Wow. That is a heavy statement. The God who formed humanity from dust wished He'd never done it in the first place. It wasn't because of a small amount of sin. No. Genesis says that *every* inclination of the human heart was *only* evil *all the time.* Perpetual evil. No remorse, no guilt. Just utter evil as far as the eye can see.

These people aren't innocently minding their own business with the occasional slipups. They are fully steeped in darkness, and that darkness has sucked every bit of life from them. They have completely handed themselves over to evil. They are dead in their sin long before God steps in. According to Jesus in John 15:1–8, it's not the live branches that are burned, only the ones who have already cut themselves off from their one source of life.

At that point, God assents to their free will and allows those intent on destruction to die in their sin. At the same time, He pursues Noah and his family, the only ones not fully engulfed in evil, through His protection of them. God is heartbroken at the state of humanity, but to preserve it, He has to save humanity from itself. It isn't the first time, and it's far from the last.

Remember, God promises that humanity's Savior will be the offspring of the woman (Genesis 3:15), and He is going to see that promise through.

When God floods the earth with heaviness and regret, He has to clear death to make way for life. Just like firefighters deal with a forest environment inundated with dead branches, God must do something to protect and pursue the good of the organisms that are still alive. In other words, the inhabitants of earth in the times of Noah aren't just running from God or going through a season of rebellion. They rebel so much and so wholly that sin—death—overtakes them entirely.

God doesn't save Noah and his family because they are perfect. It isn't Noah's perfection that makes him worthy of God's protection. He is far from perfect. At one point, Noah gets so drunk and naked that his own son Ham somehow disgraces him (Genesis 9:20–25). Noah's faith saves him, and by it he becomes an "heir of the righteousness that is in keeping with faith" (Hebrews 11:7).

If you think I'm doing hermeneutical gymnastics here, look at the covenant God makes with Noah after the flood:

> "And from each human being, too, I will demand an accounting for the life of another human being.
>
> "Whoever sheds human blood,
> by humans shall their blood be shed;
> for in the image of God
> has God made mankind. . . .

> "I establish my covenant with you: Never again will all life be destroyed by the waters of a flood; never again will there be a flood to destroy the earth." (Genesis 9:5–6, 11)

God's solution to humanity's depravity is to salvage what is still alive and then make a new covenant to right what went wrong. Why, then, is this piece about shedding human blood so central to the covenant? Think about it. Based on the terms of the covenant God makes with Noah, we can infer that murder and a blatant disregard for the sanctity of human life—for the image of God—were rampant in the antediluvian world. It was a culture of death and bloodshed. This world was corrupt, dark, and fraught with suffering and pain. Far from going on some divine power trip, God mercifully wipes out the perversity that humanity had embraced so that He can ensure humanity's survival. Most striking of all, God permanently disrupts this cycle of moral decay and destruction by sending His Son to redeem and save the world for all time and history. After the floodwaters recede, God sets a rainbow in the clouds as a sign of His dedication to this redemption and says: "Whenever I bring clouds over the earth and the rainbow appears in the clouds, I will remember my covenant between me and you and all living creatures of every kind. Never again will the waters become a flood to destroy all life" (Genesis 9:14–15).

Fast-forward a bit and you will find that nevertheless, Israel later goes into exile on two separate occasions because of its rebellion against God. The book of Hosea is one of God's final attempts to wake the Northern Kingdom of Israel before the impending Assyrian exile. But they don't wake up. God's people are conquered and taken away with their tails between their legs because they got distracted by other gods and false idols. Referring to this exile, the prophet Jeremiah writes, "I gave faithless Israel her certificate of divorce and sent her away because of all her adulteries. Yet I saw that her unfaithful sister Judah had no fear; she also went out and committed adultery" (Jeremiah 3:8). That doesn't sound like God's steadfast love. That sounds like turning away and giving up. Did God really abandon His people forever?

No, not forever. For a short time and for their own good? Yes.

> Although they claimed to be wise, they became fools and exchanged the glory of the immortal God for images made to look like a mortal human being and birds and animals and reptiles.
>
> Therefore God gave them over in the sinful desires of their hearts to sexual impurity for the degrading of their bodies with one another. They exchanged the truth about God for a lie, and worshiped and served created things rather than the Creator—who is forever praised. Amen.
>
> . . . Although they know God's righteous decree that those who do such things deserve death, they not only continue to do these very things but also approve of those who practice them. (Romans 1:22–25, 32)

We see it again: God's exile of Israel is another necessary controlled burn. Not of the living, but of the dead—those who, with all the knowledge and experience of God's glory, choose to embrace death over life. However, this time of exile is also an act of discipline and God's attempt to show Israel the fruits of her rebellion and to win her back to Himself. He isn't cutting His people off and leaving forever; He is cutting them off so they can see what godlessness truly means (Hosea 5:15–6:3).

As long as we live—flawed and rebellious though we may be—God intends our restoration. As long as a single spark of life remains, God wants to win us back. Just look at what He says in Jeremiah 3:12:

> "Return, faithless Israel," declares the LORD,
> "I will frown on you no longer,
> for I am faithful," declares the LORD,
> "I will not be angry forever."

God never stops pursuing, but God does allow us to experience the consequences of our own actions as an act of *restoration*. We want to believe that pursuit will always feel warm and fuzzy, but God cares too much to share us with those things that threaten our destruction, whether those are idols we choose (like Israel's) or the culture of destruction surrounding us (like Noah's). No one is denying the hard parts of the Bible and the way it sometimes appears that God walks away. No one is saying you should shut up, sit down, and stop asking questions about the acts of destruction apparently sanctioned by God Himself. But don't miss the forest because you're looking at a few trees. Forest fires are hard to watch, mostly because God wired us to cultivate life. Sometimes, though, we need to learn to identify a prescribed fire and trust that it will bring about greater, better, healthier flourishing for all the life that remains.

The overarching witness of Scripture is essential to make sense of it all. While we might struggle to understand God's judgment, particularly in the Old Testament, we must remember that Scripture culminates in the life, death, and resurrection of Jesus, who came to reconcile all creation to the Father. Jesus is the offspring of the woman foretold in Genesis 3, and He is the one who crushes the head of the serpent once and for all. He fulfills and proves every covenant God made with human beings in all history; in Him, we have proof that God did bear the full burden of the covenant we broke. He could have chosen to condemn humanity for eternity, "but God shows his love for us in that while we were still sinners, Christ died for us" (Romans 5:8 ESV).

And He isn't done yet.

> And I heard a loud voice from the throne saying, "Look! God's dwelling place is now among the people, and he will dwell with them. They will be his people, and God himself will be with them and be their God. 'He will wipe every tear from their eyes. There will be no more death' or mourning or crying or pain, for the old order of things has passed away."
>
> He who was seated on the throne said, "I am making everything new!" (Revelation 21:3–5)

The book of Revelation tells the story of cosmic final redemption and restoration. While Israel is the key player in how God chose to tell this story in human history, this narrative is for the good of us all. The flood was never a divine act of "I'll show you!"; it was a necessary protection of and provision for the life that remained. Exile, as much as it may look like God abandoning His people, is actually a picture of how God disciplines and fights for His people against their own idols and their own unfaithfulness. And it sets the stage for Jesus—the Warrior King and Redeemer whom exiled Israel cried out for, and the fulfillment of God's promise to never destroy all creation again.

In our finite vision, we may be tempted to accuse God of giving up and ceasing His pursuit, but the story isn't over yet. We don't know how and who He will pursue or how He will win people back, but He is coming back. Death couldn't hold Him in the grave. Why would we think that death could hold Him back from *us*, His image bearers, the objects of His *khesed* love? Burning away the death that surrounds us is an act of mighty sovereign pursuit, even if it doesn't look or feel like it. It is an act of merciful, holy, righteous love.

PART 2

THIS CHANGES EVERYTHING

WHAT DOES IT MEAN FOR YOUR LIFE IF GOD IS PURSUING YOU?

See what great love the Father has lavished on us, that we should be called children of God! And that is what we are!
(1 John 3:1)

Knowing that the God of heaven actively seeks you frees you to live a life of peace and joy, from the way you think about your needs to the way you understand your own identity. In this section, we're taking all our biblical knowledge about what it means to be pursued by God and figuring out exactly what that means for our day-to-day. Do you struggle with loneliness? God draws near, and He won't ever stop. Do you fight anxiety that suggests the needs of tomorrow won't be met? God, giver of all good gifts, woos your heart through His provision, and He won't give up. Because of God's pursuit, you are profoundly safe, forever held, and always wanted. In all this loneliness and anxiety, you will find victory, even in the darkness.

If God really is pursuing you, and if He always has been . . . well, that changes everything.

CHAPTER 5

FREEDOM IN HIS NET

Have you ever known someone who struggled with drug addiction?

I have.

This friend was fun and carefree, albeit with a pronounced rebellious streak and a little too much confidence. We'd known each other for years, running in the same circles for much of our lives. As he got older, his rebellious streak manifested in a classic party phase, something so many of us went through when our lives revolved around our friendships and peers, and when the innate need to differentiate ourselves from our parents loomed so large. During that season, no one in our group of friends was shocked when he consistently drank more than everyone else, and we mostly just rolled our eyes and shook our heads when we heard the crazy stories of the trouble he'd gotten himself into. "That guy is wild," we'd say. He seemed so carefree, so quick to laugh, and so unrestricted. We didn't think he was ever in any actual danger.

Years later, older but still wild, he added new substances. Stronger and more expensive ones. Our friend group didn't talk about what he was using, but we saw all the signs. We knew his drug use was getting worse. While the rest of us grew up, going to bed early so we could get up for our corporate jobs and staying in on weekends, he was still at it—never turning down a drink or a night at the bars.

My priorities had changed long ago, but a little part of me envied the way my friend held on to his youth. "Young, wild, free," he liked to say, tongue in cheek. He was so intent on enjoying his life and so committed to maintaining his freedom, while the rest of us were settling into boring routines of coffee breaks and bill paying. Yet around this time the wild stories got a little less funny and a little more concerning. We started to wonder, *Is this normal? Does he have a real problem?* But we figured he would outgrow it the way the rest of us had. Maybe he was just a little behind.

But he didn't grow out of it.

The bags under his eyes darkened. His skin was somehow paler every time I saw him. His body couldn't keep up with the highs he was constantly pursuing, and his health started to decline, along with his ability to maintain healthy relationships. He now needed a substance to be able to laugh. His exuberance for life had faded away. Eventually, when I tried to talk to him, it felt like he had nothing left in him. It was like talking to a robot. All the light in his eyes was gone. And his choices only caused more and more damage.

He didn't have a career path, or a job that claimed forty hours of his week plus commute time. He didn't have a significant other telling him what to do and imposing her emotional needs on him. He didn't have a mortgage and the oppressively high interest rate to go along with it. He didn't have tiny humans crawling all over him first thing in the morning, stealing his sleep, and monopolizing his time. That's freedom, right?

Right?

Of course not. It was clear he wasn't free.

What started out masquerading as his lack of inhibition turned out to be a desperate need for healthy boundaries. What looked like living life to the fullest eventually left my friend with very little in his life. What seemed to be freedom was a prison he couldn't escape.

That's how addiction operates.

I remember facing something similar. Just a few months into the thick of my eating disorder, one of my close friends called to check on me, noting that a mutual friend had said of me, "It's like she lost the light in her eyes."

Whereas my friend chose the counterfeit freedom of drugs, I chose to hang my happiness on my ability to be thin and others' admiration of it. I all but removed God from how I understood my identity. I didn't want *God's* version of freedom and joy, in which I could eat full meals in good company and release control over each calorie. I didn't understand that my worth was already set. I thought I had to create my own worth and value. For a time, I thought I was free. But it was just as counterfeit as my friend's so-called freedom in his drug addiction.

Human beings love freedom, don't we? Whether we turn to drugs and alcohol or to money, beauty, youth, control, you name it, we want to be the masters of our own fate and the arbiters of our own happiness. We desperately desire abundance on our own terms. It never ends well. Because it takes us into idolatry every time.

True freedom is found when we submit to the pursuit of God and receive abundant life according to His blueprint.

In Scripture, abundant life may not look like what we expect it to. It often comes from the most unexpected places: In Christ, a cross that represented torture and empire becomes a symbol of grace and love. The last shall become first, and those who elevate themselves will be sent to the back of the line. The Lion that tears us away from idols, with their claws sunk so deep in us that we can't tell where they end and our own flesh begins, is our Savior coming to carry us away and restore us to life. Freedom is found not in total autonomy but within the parameters God has set for human flourishing.

What might look like constricting and controlling limitations set by God are sources of freedom. Closeness to God on His terms is the only way to truly live.

When Israel ran from God, He knew she was running into

her own destruction, a prison of her own making. So He set about rescuing her:

> "Ephraim is like a dove,
> easily deceived and senseless—
> now calling to Egypt,
> now turning to Assyria.
> When they go, I will throw my net over them;
> I will pull them down like the birds in the sky.
> When I hear them flocking together,
> I will catch them." (Hosea 7:11–12)

God gets up, grabs His net, and comes after us. God pursues us to catch us and keep us within the boundary lines He has set for our good. I like this visual, because I often find myself conceiving of God's precepts and principles—God's boundaries for us—as those famous stone tablets, monolithic and cold, that we find in Exodus. To be caught in God's net is a hard, painful thing. To be allowed to run toward our own destruction, though, is the real tragedy. Here we see God's desire for intimacy moved to its feet, and this time He throws His net over us to keep us from our own destruction.

Freedom without the constraints of a relationship isn't freedom at all. But to be held close and embraced tightly by a God who refuses to give up on you? Limitless power and freedom are found there in His hands. While some may reject the idea that we need God so we can be truly free, most struggle to argue against the idea that social contracts (the constraints of a relationship) are the basis of society. Even the most committed secularist would agree that the human species would have died out long ago were it not for the institution of marriage making way for stable households and child-rearing. While the married person may admit that their freedom was perhaps initially compromised by the commitment to remain faithful for richer and for poorer, in sickness and in health, the ultimate result is a greater degree of security, which leads to a higher degree of peace and joy and, yes, freedom.

Just look at the data. In a recent example, a nearly fifty-year-long study at the University of Chicago surveyed adults in the United States about their overall happiness levels. Marriage correlated with higher happiness levels more than any other factor. According to this analysis, married people are thirty percentage points happier than unmarried people. While researchers are unsure about the exact causality for this difference, we can at least safely infer that marriage, as a contract or covenant, offers something profoundly beneficial to human flourishing. The statistics indicate that monogamy does not deserve its bad rap as the archaic, limiting institution some believe it to be.[1]

The inherent paradox of flourishing and freedom is why so many people who make freedom their goal end up alone, clawing at fulfillment and success. Freedom isn't a lack of restriction; it's the ability to rest and enjoy what you have. Without commitment, we are alone. Without a covenant, we are unsafe, prone to abandonment at any moment. Without boundaries around us and constraints to limit us, every good thing we manage to obtain becomes its own idol. That was certainly the case for my friend with the drug addiction, and it was certainly the case for me with my eating disorder.

When God throws His net over us, He does not do so because He wants to imprison and control us. It's because wise boundaries and rightly ordered worship are the keys to our joy. Our freedom is within His net. Only in total surrender to God will we find the fullness of life we are after. He waits for our hearts and calls us back to who we are, and then He turns us loose to serve Him with lives of true freedom and power. James 1:25 says, "But whoever looks intently into the perfect law that gives freedom, and continues in it—not forgetting what they have heard, but doing it—they will be blessed in what they do."

Lest you still struggle with the idea that seeking unmitigated freedom apart from Christ could possibly be a bad thing, I want to reiterate: We never run from God to other things that then lead to our thriving. Those other things we're running to? They will only enslave us. They are idols that will always hurt us in the end.

Don't believe me? Tell me what you think freedom means. Say aloud what you think you need to love your life and love yourself. I bet a few of these come to mind: wealth, a "good" body, a significant other, a high-powered career, a degree, a house, an enviable vacation plan, a good drink, or the fulfillment of all your ambitions. Our ideas of abundance revolve around these temporary things. But the truth is that none of these things will bring you happiness for long; every desire on that list will master you in time.

Pastor and bestselling author Timothy Keller puts it this way:

> The claim is that Jesus is the only master, the only thing to live for that will not exploit you. And here is why. We observed that love relationships require the loss of independence but that both parties must give it up together. You must say to the other person: "You first. I will adjust for you, I will give up my freedom for you, I will sacrifice for you." However, both parties must say that. If only one person does that and not the other, that is exploitation. . . . Christianity is the only religion that claims God gave up his freedom so we could experience the ultimate freedom—from evil and death itself. Therefore, you can trust him. He sacrificed his independence for you, so you can sacrifice yours for him. And when you do, you will find that it is the ultimate, infinitely liberating constraint.[2]

We understand this tension when it comes to the legal system. Most of us agree to follow certain rules (aka laws) that, when implemented properly, ensure a higher degree of safety and success. For example, we agree that speed limits on highways decrease the likelihood of severe collisions. We agree that big corporations should not be allowed to exploit private citizens. We agree that it is wrong to take the life of another person, and if someone does kill another person, they need to face consequences. All of us give up a certain amount of freedom for a greater good.

Boundaries, from the large-scale legal ones to the deeply personal ones we set for our own behavior, enable flourishing. In an award-winning 2006 study, a landscape-architecture student assessed the impact of fences around children's play areas. The researcher looked at classes of children at recess and analyzed their behavior under different circumstances. The findings were fascinating, albeit intuitive to anyone with children: When the kids had a fence surrounding their playground, they ran around independently, up to the fence, playing and exploring without fear. When they were sent to recess in an unfenced outdoor space, the kids "huddled around their teacher," apparently nervous about the lack of structure and—yep, you guessed it—boundaries.[3] Paradoxically, fences don't limit exploration; they foster it. Likewise, boundaries don't limit freedom. They enable humans to truly experience it.

In Galatians 3 Paul makes an interesting observation: God's covenant with Abraham to bless the world through his seed (which he points out as being singular because it refers to Jesus, the Savior of the world) was made more than four hundred years before Moses received the law on Mount Sinai. Thus, God's faithfulness is contingent not on our ability to follow all the rules but rather on His character. So what was the purpose of the law? The law was given as a means for humans to relate to God until Jesus came to fulfill it, and it was given to offer a new way. It was meant to give humanity a picture of the way to health and flourishing, as opposed to the way that leads to death (Proverbs 14:12). According to Galatians 3:21–22, while the law was not the vehicle for human salvation or "able to impart life" (NASB), it was a necessary mnemonic to help humans understand the destructiveness of evil and the impossibility of achieving our own righteousness. It "locked up everything under the control of sin" (NIV), meaning it highlights every place we fall short of God's perfection in our own strength. The law lays the groundwork and provides necessary context for the Savior who is to come.

> Is the law, therefore, opposed to the promises of God? Absolutely not! For if a law had been given that could impart life, then righteousness would certainly have come by the law. But Scripture has locked up everything under the control of sin, so that what was promised, being given through faith in Jesus Christ, might be given to those who believe. (Galatians 3:21–22)

Within God's boundaries for us, there is a divine generosity. He doesn't trip us up and humiliate us for the sake of asserting His superiority; He teaches us through our errors and edifies us through our failures. Likewise, the net He throws over His people in Hosea is not the weapon of a hunter intent on capture and death. God's very heart is tied to their flourishing. No, the net God throws over them is to prevent them from flying away from His abundance and into the open sky of their own ignorance and the destruction that comes from serving false gods.

What we learn from the net is that even when our hearts rebel and our actions follow suit, God will still fight for closeness with us. The net is uncomfortable—perhaps even painful. Within it, though, we find ultimate safety.

We can't run. We can't escape. Whereas the human heart is wired to idolize freedom and flee from difficult realities, God will tether us to truth and ask us to face the challenges we would otherwise run from. In the net, God's grace approaches our rebellion. He meets us there. He enters the captivity we chose or stumbled into; He captures us with His love to prevent us from being captured by death.

> But each of us was given grace according to the measure of Christ's gift. Therefore it is said,
>
> "When he ascended on high he made captivity
> itself a captive;
> he gave gifts to his people."
>
> (When it says, "He ascended," what does it mean but that he had also descended into the lower parts of the earth? He who descended is the same one who ascended far above all the heavens, so that he might fill all things.) (Ephesians 4:7–10 NRSV)

Jesus turns captivity on its head; to be captive to Christ is to be truly free. To be caught in God's net is to be wholly liberated. God descends into our existential gridlock to break us free with His own two hands. But He doesn't just unlock the prison door; He restores our ability to experience freedom by setting us free from sin itself. As a result, we are caught up in the paradox of being "slaves" (as Romans 6 puts it) to God and receiving the grace and eternal life He offers freely. In effect, we are slaves to freedom, constrained by boundaries that impart total peace, all-surpassing joy, and limitless abundance. Our understanding of true freedom has to change when we grasp what Jesus has liberated us from and what He has freed us to do.

For my friend with the drug addiction, liberation eventually came through limits. One night he was caught with illegal drugs on him (along with illegal weapons to protect those drugs), and for these offenses, he landed in court-ordered rehab. In the confines of the rehab facility, he was provided with the resources to detox from the substances that had been controlling his life. Without his go-to form of escape, he finally found freedom (because escape and freedom are not the same thing). I'm sure that, for a moment, he felt like he had been caught in a net. But that net was what led to his restoration into full life and into freedom. The chains of his addiction were broken while he was in captivity.

Tell me: What are you running from? Why are you afraid of the goodness God wants to lavish on you? The dreams in your heart were put there by Him, and He has a plan to fulfill them. The idol glittering in the distance is just metal rendered by human hands, with no power to save or fulfill you. When God confounds your plans to run toward the idol and catches you in His net, see that for what it is: His loving, protective pursuit of your heart. In the world we live in—where autonomy and individualism are the highest goods, where following your heart might as well be a moral imperative—being caught by Christ might initially feel like oppression, but it's the furthest thing from it.

Listen to Jesus and hear the care in His voice: "For whoever wants to save his life will lose it; but whoever loses his life for My sake will find it. For what good will it do a person if he gains the whole world, but forfeits his soul? Or what will a person give in exchange for his soul?" (Matthew 16:25–26 NASB).

In His boundaries—in His net—are true abundant life and deep abiding rest. Because of God's pursuit, you can experience life to the fullest and maintain your soul.

CHAPTER 6

YOU ARE WANTED

Growing up, I packed a giant trunk every summer and headed to camp in southwest Missouri for four weeks of outdoor activities and learning about the Bible. The summer when I was fourteen, I found myself in something of a love triangle. Well, it felt like a love triangle. I think a better description is that I observed from the sidelines a budding romance between my friend and the boy I liked, wishing all the while that I was the romantic interest. The boy in question? Brink. I am not changing his name because it's entirely too fitting, and because I spent twenty minutes trying to find him on social media with no success. So I think I am safe.

(This message is for Brink: If by some wild turn of events you are reading this now, I look forward to getting your feedback. Before you read this, I need to make the earth-shattering confession that I had an underwhelming crush on you in 2006. I hope this news doesn't make you question all your life choices to this point. If so, I am truly sorry, but our love was not meant to be. All my best.)

Brink, as his name suggests, looked like an early 2000s Disney Channel Original Movie heartthrob come to life. He had bright blue eyes and a hair swoop that defied the Missouri humidity, and, of course, he was a football player. I, along with every girl in my cabin that summer, vied for his attention.

He was in my grade, so my cabin of girls and his cabin of boys were paired for several activities throughout the summer. From the start, he was clearly interested in my confident, athletic friend Mary Louise. I knew I was at a disadvantage, but I still did everything in my power to get his attention without being too obvious. I did a full face of makeup each time I thought we would see him. I tried to be funny and a little flirtatious. I tried to show interest without being desperate. But it was Mary Louise who got letters full of inside jokes from him every few days.

My journal from that summer reads: "I feel so overlooked, so second-best. I don't know why I am not good enough for a guy like that." I remember crying hot tears into my pillow, but it wasn't really about Brink. Truthfully, he wasn't even my type. He wasn't all that funny, and he wasn't all that kind. So many years and so much brain development later, I giggle at the melodramatic journal entries and the outsized teenage feelings over a guy I didn't even really care about. Now I can see what was really going on beneath the surface: I was crying because the feeling of being *unseen* hit something deep, and it hurt. Worse than not getting the attention in the first place was realizing that I had put on my very best show and it still wasn't working. I did feel unseen, and I wasn't a fan of being second-best.

I've spent a lot of my life trying to avoid ever feeling that way again. I did everything I could to make sure I wouldn't be overlooked. Sometimes that looked like changing my appearance (which you may have guessed). Sometimes that looked like making sure I seemed smart or qualified. It has often looked like remaining aloof, holding my cards close to my chest, and trying to fake it till I make it in any situation—at least they'd keep wondering for a while before they realized I wasn't that special after all.

For a while, I thought I had conquered my fear of being unseen. And then God decided to give me a small platform on Instagram to write devotionals, initially for young adult women. So many people erroneously believe that becoming viral on the internet and having thousands of followers will finally validate them and make them feel seen. I fear the Lord gave me my platform specifically to let you know that it doesn't work that way. The goalpost will always move. For every follower I have, it seems like ten more people think I am a stupid girl with weak theology, and even more people simply don't care at all (the latter is somehow worse). For all its good, social media is a daily, if not hourly, in-my-face reminder of all the people who don't desire *me*, and they will never ask me to sit at their table because they don't see anything worthwhile in me. I would be lying if I told you I haven't cried many tears because I've so often felt like an outsider looking in, wondering why I'm so easily overlooked by the many Christian in-groups in this space. These tears are just like the hot tears that rolled down my face all those years ago at summer camp, as I wondered what was wrong with me that made it so easy to look right past me to someone else.

I confess even now that when I can tell I have been written off or dismissed, that familiar twinge of pain is often immediately followed by a familiar desire: to prove them wrong. *I don't need their approval or their attention*, I say to myself. *I will show them. I will find a way to do something incredible that they can't ignore. They'll be sorry!*

Have you ever felt that way? So determined to be seen that your whole life becomes about proving you are desirable to other people? I find that most of us have at least one big wound, likely from childhood, that dictates much of our behavior even in adult life. Maybe someone told you that you weren't very smart as a child, and it still really hurts when you feel like you don't have the right answers. Perhaps eight-year-old you overheard a relative calling you "a little chubby," and ever since, you have been dieting and exercising to the point of exhaustion, just so you can be seen as thin. I know many people in the world feel neglected, even abandoned, by one or both parents—physically, emotionally, or otherwise—and their entire lives seem to be defined by that wound and the intense drive to never let that happen again.

The wound of being unseen is one that frames many of our lives. And I have beautiful news for us today: To be pursued by God means that you are profoundly wanted. You are not second-string. You are not overlooked. God pursues you, specifically and intentionally, because He is crazy about you. To be pursued by God is to be fully seen for all of who you are—the good and the bad—and to be fully desired. But He doesn't stop there. He comes after you over and over because He loves you.

God chooses *you*.

To help your heart believe it, we're going to the Song of Songs. I won't lie to you: This book of the Bible can feel esoteric. It's a love poem between a young man and young woman in ancient Israel that offers a window into their courtship and union. Throughout history, this book of the Bible has confused people, because it doesn't offer a neat lesson or conclusion and it honestly gets graphic. We can read this book of the Bible at a high level as being primarily a poem about a healthy romantic relationship, full of joy and free from shame, within the context of marriage. Because marriage as a sacrament is a picture of how Christ loves the church (take a look at Ephesians 5 and Revelation 19), the Song of Songs also paints a beautiful picture of God's pursuit of His beloved.

For those of us who have felt overlooked and second-best time and time again, reading the Song of Songs offers a much needed reminder of just how much and how deeply God loves you. The woman in the Song of Songs, sometimes referred to as the Shulamite, seems to be familiar with these feelings of unworthiness too. She notes her insecurity straightaway in chapter 1:

> Do not stare at me because I am dark,
> because I am darkened by the sun.

My mother's sons were angry with me
and made me take care of the vineyards;
my own vineyard I had to neglect.
(Song of Songs 1:6)

"Do not look at me," she says. In a time when dark skin was associated with hard physical labor, light skin was seen as desirable and beautiful. Because her brothers mistreated her and forced her to work outside, her skin darkened. She took care of others' vineyards and didn't have the time or ability to tend to her own appearance.

Early in her life, she was told exactly what she was good for—work. That work darkened her skin and changed how she saw herself. It made her shy away when others gazed upon her. Her true value and dignity lay unseen and overlooked, even by her own family; indeed, this work made this young woman afraid to be truly seen.

I know what it feels like to have been hurt enough times that you become afraid of yet another wound or bit of evidence that confirms what you already feel deeply: You are not enough. Rather than subject yourself to more rejection and more pain, you start to hide yourself, whether by trying to change your personality or your appearance (as I am prone to do), or by withdrawing altogether.

You know who isn't fooled or deterred by your best attempts to hide away? Jesus.

Listen! My beloved!
Look! Here he comes,

leaping across the mountains,
bounding over the hills.
My beloved is like a gazelle or a young stag.
Look! There he stands behind our wall,
gazing through the windows,
peering through the lattice.
My beloved spoke and said to me,
"Arise, my darling,
my beautiful one, come with me."
(Song of Songs 2:8–10)

Just like the lover in the Song of Songs, Jesus climbs mountains and runs miles to be with you. He descends all the way from heaven to take on human flesh and show you that He would do anything for you. He comes to call out the beauty that has been within you all along and to take you with Him. He is strong, and He is determined. He sees past the wounds that have almost defined you, past the pain that looms large in the way you understand yourself. He sees you. He loves you. He thinks you are so beautiful and so extraordinary that He bounds over hills to get to you.

Most of all, the Song of Songs illustrates Christ and His bride, the church. And the Bible is God's redemptive plan for all creation. But remember that you are a member of that body; you are part of His creation. You are Christ's beloved. The Good Shepherd leaves the ninety-nine in pursuit of one little sheep gone astray. While this may seem like an overly individualized reading of these texts, I believe an exclusively corporate reading of the Bible is an overcorrection. The amazing thing isn't just that Jesus feels so passionate and enamored with me and me alone; the amazing thing is that we serve a Savior who feels so passionate and enamored with each one of us, personally *and* corporately. The gospel is encompassing and global, but God chooses to contextualize it in the lives of individuals just like you and me. The story isn't about you. It's about Him. But it is *for* you. It's okay to read it as such.

Philip Ryken offers a beautiful reflection on the Song of Songs in his book *The Love of Loves in the Song of Songs*:

> Sometimes we are tempted to think that somehow we are beneath God's notice or to imagine that we have done something so wrong (maybe something sexual) that God could never love us again, or to conclude on the basis of our present troubles that God is not for us but against us. If this is what we think, then we need to hear—once again—the truth that establishes our identity and determines our destiny: we are loved with an everlasting love. Undying love led the Son of God to leap past galaxies and bound through space to become a lowly human being on little planet Earth. Jesus came to win a lover's heart, whatever the cost. In the stirring words of one famous old hymn, "From heav'n he came and sought her, / to be his holy bride; / with his own blood he bought her, / and for her life he died."[1]

The everlasting love of Jesus forever finds us wherever we try to hide, and it sees us despite the wounds we bear. He sees you, and He pursues you even now.

I once heard the story of a woman who worked for a couple as a domestic servant. She was far from her homeland, and she didn't have many other options. At one point, she was forced to have sex with the husband because the wife couldn't have kids and hoped they could claim her baby as their own. When she did get pregnant, the wife realized she was jealous. It was too hard to have her around. The wife treated her so badly that she ran away into the desert, pregnant and alone. She had been abused and exploited. She had not been treated with the dignity she was entitled to as a bearer of God's image. Every time I remember her story, my blood boils.

Her name is Hagar. As we discussed in chapter 1, her abusers are Abram and Sarai, progenitors of God's people acting from a place of unbelievable faithlessness because God hadn't granted them their promised child yet. Abram and Sarai acted sinfully and faithlessly in their treatment of Hagar, and the Bible is transparent about that. But God pursues Hagar into the desert because God sees her. God values her. God wants her good.

Genesis 16 tells us, "The angel of the Lord found Hagar near a spring in the desert; it was the spring that is beside the road to Shur. And he said, 'Hagar, slave of Sarai, where have you come from, and where are you going?'" (verses 7–8). There in the desert, God promises to give Hagar hope and a future. God gives Hagar a way forward. Even though Hagar does not mother the nation of Israel, Abram and Sarai must reckon with their actions: Ishmael, Hagar's baby boy, is even recognized as an ancestor of the prophet Muhammad by many Muslim people.[2] Isn't that wild? The origin of so much contention between the descendants of Ishmael and the descendants of Isaac is, in one sense, Abram and Sarai's lack of faith and subsequent abuse of Hagar. God sees the injustice, and He does not glaze over it but puts their names into history forever.

To Hagar, He is *El Roi*—the God who sees (Genesis 16:13). She has been hurt, but God restores her dignity. He has a plan for her too, and for the son she was forced to conceive and then punished for bearing. God finds her in the desert and speaks tenderly to her. It isn't the last time either. On another occasion, Sarah is once again insecure about God's promises and vindictive as a result, so she tells Abraham to send Hagar and Ishmael into the desert. When they run out of water in the hot sun, Hagar heartbreakingly sets her boy under a bush and walks a short distance away, knowing that his death is imminent and she is unable to watch it.

> God heard the boy crying, and the angel of God called to Hagar from heaven and said to her, "What is the matter, Hagar? Do not be afraid; God has heard the boy crying as he lies there. Lift the boy up and take him by the hand, for I will make him into a great nation." (Genesis 21:17–18)

Ishmael's earthly father abandons him, but God doesn't. He sees Ishmael because He first saw Hagar.

God draws us out and calls us to come away with Him, just like the lover calls to the Shulamite, his beloved. God speaks love over us and restores our identity, even in the desolate, merciless desert. To really feel seen by the God of the universe, we sometimes must flee the noise. We must quiet all the distractions that numb our insecurity and hurt, even though that means feeling it all and risking the possibility of being hurt once more. Maybe that means deleting the app that, despite offering a quick flood of dopamine on demand, often sends you spinning into comparison and a feeling of worthlessness. Maybe that means canceling your packed social calendar for an entire weekend to spend time in solitude with the Lord and make space to hear Him speak. Maybe that means setting down the bottle of wine, knowing that the fuzzy warmth it gives is simply a temporary anesthetic offering relief from the anxiety or conflict that God is calling you to face. What you will always find, I promise, is that God truly sees you. He desires you. He wants you. He perceives the good and beautiful in you, and He will vanquish the darkness that lurks within you too.

"Arise, my darling, my beautiful one, come with me" (Song of Songs 2:10). Hear His invitation to be with Him in the wilderness as the beautiful proposal that it has always been.

CHAPTER 7

PURSUED BY THE GOD WHO PROVIDES

Looking at the hospital bill in my hand, I felt my heart drop to the floor. My husband, Tanner, and I were new parents living in Orange County, California, and, like a lot of people in 2020, we were facing a financially tough year. Due to the pandemic, I took a series of pay cuts and Tanner, though thankfully still employed as a college and young adult pastor, was still earning a ministry salary. I had just given birth to our baby boy, Judah, a couple of months earlier, and we'd barely scraped together enough money for the labor and delivery bills.

But now we had even more hospital bills, ones we

hadn't planned for and couldn't afford. I didn't know what we would do.

After Judah was born, he had trouble breastfeeding before we even left the hospital. It was the first time I'd ever tried to breastfeed, and it was really hard to get the hang of it. We were given very little lactation support, but we assumed we would figure everything out when we got home.

We did not. We made it through one night of suspiciously good sleep before we realized Judah wasn't eating enough. I was starting to spiral and feeling panicky about our new baby, so Tanner called the after-hours pediatrician line and explained our concerns. I couldn't hear what the doctor was saying, but I could see Tanner following her instructions, checking Judah's skin, mouth, and eyes. As I watched, Tanner got more and more uneasy. Then I heard, "Okay, so you think we should take him to the ER right away?" The doctor suspected that Judah, like many newborns, had low blood sugar and dehydration, both caused by his feeding struggles in those first few days.

As I bawled my eyes out, we called our families to explain that we had to go to the nearby children's hospital to get help for Judah. My parents were still in town to help us settle in as first-time parents, and I vividly remember the fear on my dad's face as he helped us get into the car. As we drove to the hospital, Judah seemed too quiet in his car seat. It was 10:00 p.m. on the Saturday before Christmas.

After arriving at the hospital, Tanner and I quickly realized two things: (1) Judah was certainly going to be admitted overnight, and (2) due to COVID-19 protocols, only one of us could stay. Of course it was going to be me. I wouldn't have wanted to be anywhere else but with my baby at that moment. Still, I was less than forty-eight hours postpartum after my first childbirth, still bleeding a ton and in a lot of pain. I was terrified, and I was also firmly convinced that I was the worst mother on earth. Sitting on a cold hard hospital chair under fluorescent lights, I watched nurses poke needles into my newborn and run test after test. He was indeed dehydrated, and his blood sugar was dangerously low. He needed an IV, phototherapy treatments for jaundice, and a rigorous feeding schedule.

I set an alarm for every hour and forty-five minutes to wake up and feed my new baby, in between trying to sleep on a tiny hospital cot and getting up almost as often to do all the postpartum things you're supposed to do (if you know, you know). I had to time every feed and report it to a nurse. I remember feeling like everyone in that hospital thought I was just as bad a mom as I did. I didn't sleep much at all, but I did pray. And pray and pray and pray.

Crying through the pain of first-time breastfeeding, I felt so helpless and desperate. I don't know that I have ever prayed a more sincere "Lord, please help" prayer in my life.

And you know what? He did help.

The miraculous thing about that night is that almost every prayer I prayed was answered within minutes.

"Lord, let his bilirubin levels go down."

At the next check, they were.

"Lord, let him get a really good feed this time."

When the nurse weighed him to see how many ounces he'd gotten, she exclaimed, "Four ounces? That can't be right."

"Lord, please help my milk come in."

And it did, within an hour of my prayer. This was difficult because I was all alone and had no idea what was supposed to happen, and it was a miraculous show of God's faithfulness to a scared and exhausted postpartum mom who just wanted to be able to feed her baby.

I will never forget my experience in that hospital. By the time I left, I had accrued enough trauma to send me into a brutal season of postpartum anxiety. Yet I was also trying to articulate how near God felt to me. How everything I needed, He provided. How it seemed that every word I spoke landed right in the center of His heart. How He was there in the room with us, just as concerned about my sweet little boy as my own dad when he had helped me get into the car earlier that night.

In Matthew 7 Jesus preaches to the crowds:

> "You parents—if your children ask for a loaf of bread, do you give them a stone instead? Or if they ask for a fish, do you give them a snake? Of course not! So if you sinful people know how to give good gifts to your children, how much more will your heavenly Father give good gifts to those who ask him." (verses 9–11 NLT)

We don't always speak to God as a father, right? When we pray, we often speak to Him like He isn't really there and doesn't really have the desire or power to help us. But in that hospital, I cried out to the Lord as the loving dad He is. Unlike my dad or Judah's own dad, who were restricted by the COVID-19 pandemic, God wasn't stuck in the waiting room. God came with me into that tiny hospital room. God pulled up a hard hospital chair right next to me. God followed me; God *pursued* me.

As proof of His pursuit—His nearness—God responded to the desperate, earnest pleas I prayed to Him, my Father in heaven. And He provided.

Does this mean that God isn't near or pursuing us when our most sincere and heartbroken prayers go unanswered the way we want them to be answered? I do think unanswered prayers should push us to examine our own motives; God isn't going to give us something that will hurt us, even if we're begging for it. He's not going to give us the snake even if we're begging for it and insisting it's a fish.

However, we have all struggled with the reality that God allows tragic, awful, evil things to happen to good people. We prayed for the healing that didn't come or the job that never materialized. We prayed for restoration, but the relationship remained broken. What do we do, then, with God's pursuit through provision?

Friend, He is the bread. He is the bread sent from heaven to sustain and save us.

> Then Jesus declared, "I am the bread of life. Whoever comes to me will never go hungry, and whoever believes in me will never be thirsty. But as I told you, you have seen me and still you do not believe. All those the Father gives me will come to me, and whoever comes to me I will never drive away. . . .

> "No one can come to me unless the Father who sent me draws them, and I will raise them up at the last day." (John 6:35–37, 44)

See that last part? God draws us toward the provision that comes through Jesus. Nearness to Him is the source and the sustenance of our lives. Should even the worst happen—physical death or ultimate betrayal or utter ruin—Jesus delivers us from all evil and darkness and ushers us into His presence. In His resurrection, He already beat death. There is no other enemy for Him to conquer. From an eternal perspective, He has provided Himself, and all the brutal things we face in our lives are but the final gasps of evil before we find unending joy and final restoration with Him. He is the bread we survive on, even in the bleakness of the world as it is now, and He will be our bread when the world is once again as it should be.

Despite the pain we may experience, utter need before God is a gift of providence. You don't realize how much God shows up for you when you're just coasting through life. Only amid desperation do we see His providence as the concrete, tangible thing that it is.

And when I was new to motherhood and struggling all the way, He wasn't done yet.

We got the bill for that ER stay a few months later: eight thousand dollars. It was more than I paid for all my prenatal care and the birth combined. "This can't be right," I said to Tanner. While we were thankful we had taken Judah that night, we also had had some issues with the care plan that drove up the cost. I prayed for a week before getting the courage to call the hospital's billing office.

I spoke to the nice woman on the phone and explained my complaints. I could hear her typing notes as she asked questions about the concerns I raised. She put me on hold for a few minutes, and my adrenaline spiked. Finally, she came back to the phone and said, "I will be discussing this with my manager, and we will send an updated bill within fourteen days." But no bill ever came. A few weeks later, I went to the hospital's online portal to check my balance: zero dollars. They had cleared our debt completely.

God reached out to us again in an act of merciful providence.

Of course, providence is more than an answer to our requests. Providence, the protective care of God, extends to our daily needs for food, water, and clothing. In modern times, it extends to our finances. When the Israelites were struggling in the desert as they made their way from Egypt to the promised land, they were totally dependent on God. God had drawn His people into the wilderness to get them out of slavery and deliver them into a land of milk and honey (Exodus 3:8), but He prepared them for the abundance ahead when they were still in the desert. While they were there, exposed and wandering, they were dependent on Him not just in the spiritual sense but for their actual bread and water. God showed Himself faithful in providing for their daily physical needs through bread from heaven.

What does it mean to have our needs met? As a woman in her thirties with two kids living in the USA, I'm tempted to think of things like fancy vacations and nice clothes and expensive date nights as needs, or as things I'm entitled to because I work hard. When we live in such comfort, and with such a high standard of what it means to be provided for, I fear that we don't live close enough to a state of raw need to know how well God takes care of us and how much He pursues us through His provision for us. He will provide food when we are hungry, water when we are thirsty, and clothes when we need covering. God will provide shelter. So long as God has ordained for us to be on this earth, He will ensure that our physical bodies continue functioning. There will be manna for each day, sustenance through the harsh wilderness. God does not expect us to muscle through our humanity; indeed, He made our human muscles too weak to sustain ourselves without Him.

> "Therefore I tell you, do not worry about your life, what you will eat; or about your body, what you will wear. For life is more than food, and the body more than clothes. Consider the ravens: They do not sow or reap, they have no storeroom or barn; yet God feeds them. And how much more valuable you are than birds! . . .
>
> "If that is how God clothes the grass of the field, which is here today, and tomorrow is thrown into the fire, how much more will he clothe you—you of little faith! And do not set your heart on what you will eat or drink; do not worry about it. For the pagan world runs after all such things, and your Father knows that you need them. But seek his kingdom, and these things will be given to you as well." (Luke 12:22–24, 28–31)

The birds don't agonize over where their next meal is coming from; the flowers don't weep when they can't afford the latest trends. In His grace and love for His creation, God has fed and clothed them. In His grace and love for you, He will do the same. We may need to align our idea of nourishment and covering with His instead of what the world says is necessary. We will need to retrain our hearts to be satisfied with perhaps simple food and clothing, and to release control over what they look like. The beauty of being satisfied with simple providence is that we get to rest. God provided extra manna for the Israelites on that sixth day so that they could enjoy total rest on the seventh. When we trust the provision He freely offers, He provides rest too.

The birds? They are content. The flowers? Better clothed than Solomon in all his splendor. When the Israelites obeyed God's command to rest in His provision, they were fully cared for even in the harshest environments and far away from home. True abundance does not come from having many things but from the abundance of God's presence and the extent to which you experience it daily (Luke 12:15).

Give God a chance to show up in the gaps. He can and will appear in those spaces of physical and financial need. He will extend His arms to you when He meets your needs.

But there is still more.

In the weeks following my hospital stay, I spiraled despite feeling God's closeness. Not for days, not for weeks, but for months. Neurologists will tell you that the brain of a newly postpartum mom undergoes massive restructuring.[1] This process is meant to be adaptive; we develop new wiring that enables us to bond with our children and react to threats and needs accordingly. It truly changes you forever. However, if something stressful or traumatic gets thrown into the mix amid all that neuroplasticity, the effects can make the notoriously difficult newborn days almost unbearable. That's what I think happened to me. It's not that I endured a particularly severe trauma, but because of what was going on in my body and brain when I was faced with my baby's first medical emergency, the trauma messed me up. I timed Judah's feeds until he was a year old. I fed him every three hours day and night, setting an alarm just to be safe. I pumped after every single feed around the clock to protect my milk supply, though it was not low at all. I donated one thousand ounces of milk that year and dumped out many, many more. Judah wouldn't take a bottle, and I was fully convinced he would need a feeding tube put in his stomach. My brain was just stuck, and I was sure that I was unable to feed my child and we would end up back in the ER.

In my emotional and spiritual need, God provided. While I was pregnant, I had somehow gotten a group of older moms to let me sit at their table for Bible study on Wednesday mornings. One of them, Natalie, had four kids, and I thought she had to be one of the best mothers in the world. She talked about all her kids like they hung the moon. She delighted in them, and they all knew it. I loved the way she parented, and that was partly why I made her hang out with me even before I had kids. After Judah was born, I was so scared to be alone with him. When Tanner had to run ministry programming one night a week, Natalie brought over dinner, held Judah, cleaned my kitchen, and talked me through all my anxieties. Another mom friend, Leah, invited me on a walk (because, FYI, getting a new mom out into the sun and fresh air is always a good call) and prayed for my anxiety in the middle of the street. My sister-in-law, conveniently also a birth doula, stopped by my house at 11:00 p.m. amid my particularly acute anxiety attack about Judah's feeding habits, sent a lactation consultant to my house and handled the payment, and booked me a massage with a therapist who heard my story and prayed over me while she worked on my exhausted shoulders.

When my own mom was far away in Colorado, these incredible women stepped into a tender space in my life and met real needs, most of which I never vocalized. God as my Shepherd, leading me forward and following me wherever my anxious mind wandered, made sure I wasn't alone. He provided for me beyond my expectations. David thought so too:

> You prepare a table before me
> in the presence of my enemies.
> You anoint my head with oil;
> my cup overflows. (Psalm 23:5)

This verse paints the stunning picture of God the Shepherd hosting a banquet for the psalmist, His sheep. In the presence of David's enemies, God set a feast. When the enemy attacked and targeted, God laid out a dinner party. While this action might be interpreted as gloating or taunting the enemy, I think there's more to it: Sitting down to a good meal in the face of attack is embracing safety and provision when every other part of us wants to run away. And the other important piece is that banquets are rarely just for a party of two.

In that season, God hosted a banquet for me, and He invited those women to sit around the table with me. Although my heart was heavy and the struggle was too much to bear at times, I was well nourished and surrounded by people who loved me well. My enemy, anxiety that darkened my thinking, and the Enemy that exploited it at every opportunity were put in their places. God uses people to provide, by His design and with deep purpose. Yes, my pliant postpartum brain was low-hanging fruit for the anxiety I fought off that year, but that same neuroplasticity is why I am sure that the ways these women nurtured me changed me forever.

So God doesn't just provide the bare minimum. God meets our basic needs, and then God desires to surround us with a wealth of community. God hosts a lavish dinner party for sheep. When you put it that way, it's almost as nonsensical as God becoming a man, leaving heaven to live among us, dying on a cross, and coming back to life so we can live in permanent peace and profound abundance. Almost.

The way God provides for us is part of how God pursues us. When you pray for help, remember that He is a good Father looking for every opportunity to respond to your earnest needs. When your physical or financial needs feel too big and too scary, remember that He will sustain you every single day He has ordained for you on this earth, just as He did for the Israelites in the desert and as He continues to do for the birds and the wildflowers. When you feel alone, remember that the Good Shepherd is preparing a banquet for you in defiance of the darkness, and He has provided you with others to surround you. His abundance is wherever He is; don't run from it. Instead, embrace the goodness and mercy following you.

CHAPTER 8

DARKNESS DOESN'T STAND A CHANCE

Warning for my fellow tender hearts out there: I'm about to talk about a pregnancy I lost in 2020. Lord knows, I went through a long season when I wouldn't have wanted to be caught unprepared for the story I am about to tell. This is your permission to skip this chapter if you need to and return to it in a few months (or maybe even years) to process with me. I'll still be here. If you choose to stay, know that I am going to cry with you. I've never written about this before; something about it felt too delicate and too sacred.

But if you need to flip ahead now, I'll tell you the main takeaway first: Darkness never wins. Darkness can't win. Jesus pursues us into the darkness. The Light of the World descends into the depths to be near us and save us, and anywhere the light goes, darkness must surrender. And in the light, Christ gives you victory.

If you're forging ahead in this chapter, we're going back to 2020. *That* 2020. Early in the year, my husband and I had finally decided to start a family, and we were aware that it could take months or longer. We knew it wouldn't be easy. Somehow, though, within a month I got that first positive pregnancy test. I pulled out my phone to document the moment, and looking at the photos now, I see fear (holy though it was) in our eyes as we thought of this monumental change ahead. And I see innocence: a pure, expectant joy. We knew the statistics around miscarriage, but before one happens to you, you don't think it'll ever happen to you.

A few weeks later, we were in a dark room with the ultrasound technician. Shortly into the appointment, her chipper, friendly tone changed. I knew. I knew right then we weren't going to leave with a cute string of photos to hang on the fridge. My heart sank. You don't think it's going to happen to you.

When my doctor came into the room a few minutes later, she explained that the baby we'd been praying over and planning around and dreaming about had died days before. For the next few minutes, she explained my options moving forward to handle the remains of the baby I already loved. Hot tears ran down my face; some were of grief, and some were of embarrassment at having the joy I had felt mere hours before.

I never felt joy like that in a pregnancy again. Sure, I was excited to be pregnant with my subsequent children, but the innocence of that excitement when you have no reason to think anything could go wrong was gone. I am still mourning it.

We decided to wait to see if my miscarriage would resolve on its own. For the next two weeks, I walked around half praying for a miracle or a miscalculation and half painfully aware of the unsuccessful life I carried within my own body. I felt like a tomb. Stone cold and solitary. This kind of grief was so novel—feeling like I housed death in my very body, wondering how could it *not* be my fault?—and yet, from a statistical standpoint, so profoundly plain. After all, one in four pregnancies end this way. And knowing that was part of the pain. It felt like walking through a graveyard, where each of the hundreds of headstones represents a loss of life and the unique grief of a family. I was absolutely knocked down by this pain that the world seemed to find commonplace, if not mundane.

On Valentine's Day, it was time. My doctor prescribed medication to force my body to release the pregnancy. I can now say with confidence that that experience was more painful than childbirth, not because of the physical sensation (though that was awful), but because there was no hope left. It was dark, and it was cold, and after that, I withdrew into myself—and the tomb I felt like.

This whole trial coincided with the beginning of the COVID-19 pandemic and a long season of isolation for the rest of the world. I want to give my 2020 self, along with anyone else who experienced tragedy in this chapter of history, the biggest hug. To fight a battle and then be forced into solitary confinement—can anyone blame us for falling apart?

Unfortunately, and also fortunately, I quickly became pregnant again by early April. Had I been able to leave my house and see a therapist, I bet they would have said something like, "Do you think maybe you should process some of your grief and anxiety around pregnancy before getting, you know, pregnant again?" That would have been great advice! Advice I should have heeded. Alas, the pandemic. I was very much not okay.

For the next nine months, I experienced a complicated, isolating paradox: I was growing life while still feeling very much like a cold, solitary tomb. Surely I'm not alone. Surely at some point you've held great blessing alongside great pain. You, too, have gotten lost in the darkness, which is made all the darker by your guilt at knowing that you should be happy. Right?

I remember crying every single day and being unable to think about anything except my fear that the baby wasn't going to be okay. I remember anxiety when I had morning sickness, and greater anxiety when I didn't. I remember feeling like no one could possibly understand. I remember wishing someone would ask what was wrong, because I couldn't figure out how to tell them. During *all that*, I had to don my mask and go to my OB appointments all by myself. Every time was like walking into the mouth of a beast. I was convinced that each appointment was going to be the bad one where I found out that I was miscarrying again.

God showed His compassion here. On the drive to one particularly nerve-wracking appointment early in my pregnancy, I wept and I prayed. I was listening to a podcast, and when it ended, for some reason, a song started playing. It began by paraphrasing

Isaiah 54:17, which says, "No weapon forged against you will prevail." The passage recounts all the examples of God's power, especially when the circumstances appear bleak. The line of the song that became a banner over my entire pregnancy says,

> I'm gonna see a victory
> For the battle belongs to You, Lord.[1]

It felt like God just wanted to let me know He was listening. That this battle wasn't mine to fight. That I could surrender all my fear to Him and trust that He holds all victory. It felt like light breaking through the darkness. The tears I cried next were not tears of victory, but they were tears that meant, "Okay, God. If You say so. What other choice do I have? You are God and I am not."

When I got to my appointment that day, my ultrasound tech shared with me that she was a Christian too. But that wasn't weird: This happens a lot when you're married to a pastor and forced to make small talk. When I shared a bit more about how I was feeling that day, she told me that she had also been through a difficult miscarriage. She squeezed my hand before she started the scan and whispered, "He knows."

Because He did. Because He was there too.

From that day on, every *single* time I drove to my OB appointments, the song "See a Victory" by Elevation Worship rang through my car stereo. If I was spiraling in my fear in church one day, that song somehow ended up in the worship set. Skeptics like me will say, "That song was big that year! Of course it was everywhere!" And that's true. But that doesn't mean God couldn't use it. That doesn't mean He can't personalize something as a show of love for you or me.

I started to see God and His kindness breaking through. He pursued me even in the darkness. That's His whole game, friend. John 8:12 says, "When Jesus spoke again to the people, he said, 'I am the light of the world. Whoever follows me will never walk in darkness, but will have the light of life.'"

Maybe the darkness you feel in your very bones is darkness you walked into willfully. Let me assure you: Me too. I remember a few key moments in my life and testimony when I didn't just stumble and fall; I chose to take that next step into the valley of the shadow of death. You know what I'm talking about, right? You ignored the nagging warning that danger was ahead. You embraced the same lie that Eve did: "God just wants to control me. These rules aren't for my good!" At times, you wondered if the ways of the world were as exciting and fun as they seemed, and this time, you let the curiosity win. You thought you were taking your destiny into your own hands in an act of brave self-possession. And like me, you found out you were wrong.

You experienced the rush of independence from God for exactly half a second before the sin took control and you realized something bigger than you had its claws deep into your flesh and was intent on your destruction. Whether it was an eating disorder or a relationship that destroyed your soul or an addiction or you name it, choosing to disconnect from the light got you nothing but darkness. Sin begets death; you learned that (again) the hard way.

I hope this chapter finds you on the other side, having another part of your testimony in hand and praising the Lord for His faithfulness and grace. If not—if you are still navigating the darkness you chose and struggling to believe that God can still love and pursue you—I want you to hear me: The Light of the World is still for you.

Look at the nation of Israel. As we learn from Hosea's calling and prophecy, the Israelites had a history of national infidelity. You know what else they had? A long history of God's persistent effort to redeem them anyway. "Oh, you think you're bad?" the Holy Spirit whispers in this text. "Remember how unworthy and unfaithful the most revered figures in Israel's history truly were. And still, My plans for their redemption prevailed." I want you to read Hebrews 11, often referred to as the "Hall of Faith." Don't just skim it. Dissect it. While we don't have a lot of information on some of the characters featured here, let's start in verse 21 and see what we learn:

> By faith Jacob, when he was dying, blessed each of Joseph's sons, and worshiped as he leaned on the top of his staff. (Hebrews 11:21)

Jacob, who lied to his legally blind father to steal his twin brother's birthright (Genesis 27)?

> By faith Joseph, when his end was near, spoke about the exodus of the Israelites from Egypt and gave instructions concerning the burial of his bones. (Hebrews 11:22)

Joseph, the same guy who gloated to his brothers about being the best among them (Genesis 37)?

> By faith Moses, when he had grown up, refused to be known as the son of Pharaoh's daughter. He chose to be mistreated along with the people of God rather than to enjoy the fleeting pleasures of sin. He regarded disgrace for the sake of Christ as of greater value than the treasures of Egypt, because he was looking ahead to his reward. By faith he left Egypt, not fearing the king's anger; he persevered because he saw him who is invisible. By faith he kept the Passover and the application of blood, so that the destroyer of the firstborn would not touch the firstborn of Israel. (Hebrews 11:24–28)

High praise for Moses, right? I seem to remember Moses having a crisis about public speaking while the God of the universe spoke directly to him through the miracle of a burning bush that was not consumed by the fire. Then there's that time he disobeyed God so severely that God barred him from entering the promised land.

> By faith the people passed through the Red Sea as on dry land; but when the Egyptians tried to do so, they were drowned. (Hebrews 11:29)

Wait a minute, the Israelites? The ones who worshiped idols and false gods time after time? The ones who ran after other lovers and broke their covenant with God so badly that He called

Hosea to marry a woman guaranteed to cheat on him, all to illustrate the depth of their rebellion? Those ones?

Yes, friend. Those ones. All of them. All these murderers and sinners and liars and cheaters. The so-called Hall of Faith isn't a tribute to saints; it's a picture of how God redeems even the gravest of sinners. God remembers His beloved ones for their victories, not for their failures. Sit with that for a minute. God remembers you the same way. No matter how many times you err, and no matter how badly, He will bring light to any darkness you turn over to Him.

That sin from your past that keeps you up at night? The secret you're keeping that no one knows? The temptation that you are constantly fighting, even now? None of that will define your story; none of that will stop the God who is running after your heart. God is wholly uninterested in our striving and our feigned perfection. God can do absolutely anything, on an astounding scale, with a heart that trusts Him to defeat the darkness we can't handle on our own.

There's this tiny blue light on a power strip in my bedroom. When the lights are on, you never see it. Right after the lights turn off, everything seems so dark that I don't notice it. But when I wake up in the middle of the night and my eyes have had a bit of time to adjust, that tiny blue light is *all* I can see. The room seems to be illuminated by that wash of blue under the bed, and I can't unsee it. On multiple occasions, I have gotten up from my bed to find a stray sweatshirt to cover it up. In the darkness, even that tiny light is *so bright*.

Maybe you've looked up at the night sky and marveled at the

myriad twinkling stars. Although roughly nine thousand stars are technically visible to the average human, the farthest one we can see with the naked eye is sixteen thousand light-years away.[2] The light you're seeing right now has been flying through space at a pace of 186,000 miles per second.

No matter where you go, light pursues you. Light follows you. Light pierces through whatever darkness you're surrounded by. That star sixteen thousand light-years away? Scientists think it's a hundred thousand times more luminous than our sun. Not only is that star powerful enough to push through thousands of light-years' worth of darkness, but it's bigger and brighter than the greatest light you've ever known. Even when the light seems dim, it's not because the darkness has won or because the darkness is more powerful. No, the light is traversing light-years and galaxies to reach you. That tiny speck that seems dim to our earthly eyes (1 Corinthians 13:12) speaks to the power and strength of the light that shines in the darkness.

Jesus is like that too. Better yet, every second brings us closer to the day when Jesus returns to reunite heaven and earth, to that moment when we will see Him face-to-face in His full luminescence. The dim specks of glory we squint to see now will grow brighter and brighter until He is before us, shining with a brilliance our human eyes won't be able to look at. "The light shines in the darkness, and the darkness has not overcome it" (John 1:5). Read it one more time. The light still shines; the darkness will not overcome it.

When your hope is in Jesus, the Light of the World, the darkness can't overcome you either. No evil perpetrated by others and no trauma you've endured can claim you as its own, for you already belong to Him and live by the light of His victory.

Because of Christ's death and resurrection, you, my friend, are not a victim—not of man and not of circumstance. The light in you overcomes the darkness around you. Even when the psalmist tried to flee from God, he was forced to admit that no depth of darkness, either of his own making or of the circumstances in this broken world, could obscure the light of God's presence.

> Where can I go from your Spirit?
>   Where can I flee from your presence?
> If I go up to the heavens, you are there;
>   if I make my bed in the depths, you are there.
> If I rise on the wings of the dawn,
>   if I settle on the far side of the sea,
> even there your hand will guide me,
>   your right hand will hold me fast.
> If I say, "Surely the darkness will hide me
>   and the light become night around me,"
> even the darkness will not be dark to you;
>   the night will shine like the day,
>   for darkness is as light to you.
>   (Psalm 139:7–12)

I know better than most that when everything looks dark, it's sometimes tempting to lie down and just go to sleep. The idea of fumbling through the darkness and trying to retrace your steps through the valley of the shadow of death is too daunting. Maybe if you just stop here and rest awhile, you'll find the resolve to get yourself back into the light tomorrow.

In a culture of relativism, where moral imperatives and directives are often taken as an affront, we've lost the ability to openly identify darkness. If we're collectively unable to name the bad, we can no longer point toward the good and toward the light. As a result, we believe we have almost no choice but to embrace victimhood. To be reductionist, I think many of us are stuck in the narrative of "I am stuck and hurt, and I don't know why," or "I am here in the darkness, and there is nothing I can do about it." If no one has the authority to make sense of evil, it's impossible to overcome it. And if we can't overcome it, we eventually surrender to it. We lie down in the deep darkness.

Even though this experience may be a cultural reality for some, others are truly victims through no choice of their own. They've been exploited by other people in ways that left deep scars. Perhaps you've endured the kinds of horrific realities that no one simply recovers from—the loss of a child or a spouse, a terminal diagnosis, a natural disaster that takes everything. I don't want to diminish that. God sees your tears and holds them close (Psalm 56:8). I also want to acknowledge that regardless of the cause of your scars, God-given victory can come gradually. Scars don't heal overnight, but that doesn't mean they aren't healing. Both can be true. Also, you can't embrace Christ, the Light of the World, and still claim the darkness through which you've walked as being fundamental to *who you are*. Embracing victimhood as a central definition of your identity is to lie down in darkness. You can't walk in eternal life and simultaneously make your home among tombs.

God wants you to rest, but not here. God wants you to lie down in green pastures beside still waters (Psalm 23:2). Not here in the dark. What you may have forgotten is that God doesn't expect you to get yourself back on track and out of the valley. He's with you as that star shining through the thick blackness, just waiting for you to see and follow Him. The light of resurrection will always overtake the darkness, even the darkness of tombs. Whether that tomb is you, your own body, or the world that is full of the dead and dying, He will rescue you. He is, *at this very moment*, shining His light for you.

PART 3

HOW WE RESPOND

WHAT DOES IT LOOK LIKE TO LIVE IN LIGHT OF GOD'S NEVER-ENDING PURSUIT OF YOU?

My heart has heard you say, "Come and talk with me."
And my heart responds, "LORD, I am coming."
(Psalm 27:8 NLT)

Surely our response to God's pursuit is not just a matter of intellectual assent. It's an active response to a God who has proven Himself faithful and shown Himself to be kind. The beautiful thing about God's pursuit is that He is the initiator, and He is the template for how to pursue well. In this final section, we are going to look at how we say yes to God's pursuit through all the ways we carry on His work. We will also dive into greater depths of what it means to know Him more.

CHAPTER 9

BOUNDARIES THAT BEAR WITH

I recently heard the story of a young Christian woman (let's call her Anna) who was paired with a non-Christian roommate. Anna, sure that God had called her to ministry, made a significant effort to connect with her roommate in hopes of eventually sharing the gospel with her. She wrote her roommate daily encouraging notes with Bible verses inside, even though her roommate never acknowledged them. She invited her roommate to church with her, sometimes multiple times per week, despite her roommate always declining. She frequently offered to pray for her if she knew her roommate had a rough week ahead. The roommate initially expressed discomfort and eventually began to show signs of resentment and frustration with Anna's offers.

In one notable incident, Anna tried to start a conversation about Jesus. The roommate burst out, "I am very uncomfortable with this, and I would like you to stop," before she stormed out of the room. Further conversations revealed that Anna's roommate felt like Anna continued to try to force Christianity on her, despite the roommate's efforts to express that she was not interested in anything religious. The roommate felt like her boundaries were being breached, and she ultimately put up walls. Anna gave up. They survived the year as roommates, but they did not stay in touch.

I think we are called to pursue people, whether that means continuing to reach out to a friend going through a hard time, persisting in our efforts to reconcile with difficult family members, or refusing to hate our enemies even when it feels good to hate them. God calls us to live with a love that lays down our life for others (John 15:13; Matthew 5:43–48). In general, our love for others is far too easily extinguished by inconvenience, let alone criticism or hatred from the people we're called to care for. Nonetheless, modeling God's pursuit cannot be an excuse for breaching healthy boundaries and disrespecting others.

Boundaries are good, necessary, and biblical. We're going to talk about why. How do we model God's pursuit of us while also respecting the autonomy and desires of another person? Furthermore, how do we ensure that we don't excuse or minimize hurtful (perhaps even abusive) behaviors from others in the interest of steadfast love and forgiveness? Trickiest of all, how do we make sure that our so-called boundaries are truly healthy and life-affirming, as opposed to excuses to maintain our comfort or justify our offense?

What do boundaries have to do with God's pursuit of His beloved? If God pursues us past the point of our own personal comfort (remember the young Lion that tears us away from our idols?), and if we are called to emulate His love in this world (1 John 4:19), we must have a solid grasp on what healthy boundaries are. An improper understanding and application of boundaries threatens to isolate all of us into comfortable, lonely bubbles where no one ever rubs us the wrong way and where we write hall passes for sinful, exploitative behavior. Worst of all, we will give up on people who challenge us, hurt our feelings, or don't respond the way we think they should.

Because we are empowered to pursue other people the way God has pursued us—with steadfast love and faithfulness—we need to revisit the cultural discourse around boundaries. We can't be the kind of people who give up when people hurt our feelings or when our efforts are unsuccessful; we also can't be the kind of people who tiptoe around difficult conversations. We have to be willing to pursue difficult people in difficult situations, just like God pursues us.

In their book *Boundaries*, Dr. Henry Cloud and Dr. John Townsend make a case for healthy boundaries, rooting them in biblical truth. "In short, boundaries are not walls," they write. "The Bible does not say that we are to be 'walled off' from others. . . . The important thing is that property lines be permeable enough to allow passing and strong enough to keep out danger."[1]

Boundaries essentially differentiate between two things. Operating more like a fence that shows where one neighbor's property line ends and the other neighbor's begins, a boundary helps human beings thrive, because they have a clear sense of their own limitations, responsibilities, and burdens. When the property line is breached, there may be some kind of fallout. Enforcing boundaries is part of how we maintain healthy relationships with one another. For example, saying, "No, it's not my responsibility to make sure you're having fun," or "I'm going to remove myself from this situation that isn't healthy for me," is an important way to establish clear boundaries and healthy relationships.

How do we honor boundaries and pursue relational health while continually committing to pursue someone? It all comes down to our motivation. God-driven pursuit doesn't mean trying to conquer or subdue other humans. Genuine pursuit is motivated by a true desire to see the other person's flourishing. Thus, pursuing others can't be about trying to modify others' behaviors or expecting others to fall in line.

In some cases, pursuing people may look like stepping back from a relationship and instead committing to fervent prayer on their behalf. We also must contend with the reality that God is sovereign over them but we are not. Without the omnipotence and complete holiness of God, we can't demand or require change from other people. Unlike what God sees, we have a limited picture of what is actually best for them. Whereas God is able and entitled to pursue someone to the point of painfully removing idols or administering consequences, we often don't have that option. So here is what we are not going to do as we pursue people:

1. We're not going to continue behaviors they have asked us to stop. We're going to show them honor and respect by changing how we try to reach them.
2. We're not going to steamroll people with what we *think* they need. We're going to listen when they speak.
3. We're not going to minimize their needs. We're going to tune in and adjust our approach accordingly.

These are examples of breached boundaries, and what do they all have in common? These behaviors center us instead of centering the good of the other person. All these boundary violations come from the angle of "I know what's best for you," instead of "I want you to truly flourish."

Screaming the gospel at people whose hearts are not ready for it does nothing but confirm their suspicions that Christians are arrogant and selfish. It does not convey the tender heart of God, who puts His own well-being on the line time after time. There are other ways, okay?

How do we show a healthy respect for boundaries while also being faithful to the call of the gospel and modeling God's pursuit of us? To quote a saying on a bracelet I had in 1998, "WWJD?" Let's look at the way Jesus handles boundaries: "Those whom I love I rebuke and discipline. So be earnest and repent. Here I am! I stand at the door and knock. If anyone hears my voice and opens the door, I will come in and eat with that person, and they with me" (Revelation 3:19–20).

Jesus left heaven, took on flesh, endured false accusations, suffered torture and brutal death, defeated hell, came back to life, and then ascended to heaven, where He sits at the right hand of the Father until He returns to restore both heaven and earth. He did all that for you. Yet instead of barging through the door to tell you the good news or assert His true authority, He stands at the door and *knocks*. He doesn't force entry. In Revelation 3 Jesus speaks to the church in Laodicea. This is the famously lukewarm church that Jesus threatens to spit out of His mouth! During that scathing rebuke, Jesus still affirms that His discipline is the overflow of His love for them. But Jesus, ready with this discipline, stands at the door and knocks, patiently awaiting their repentance.

The goal is that others will live fully alive, with Jesus at the center of their lives. When you build enough trust and relational equity, I believe you will get an opportunity to share your whole heart. But it's always going to be a process. If someone asks you to stop sharing verses, you can pivot! Start bringing them coffee or ice cream instead, at least for now. If someone doesn't want to talk about faith, you can build trust in that relationship by talking about other things until they start asking questions. I believe we can trust God to bring about these opportunities when we commit to the slow, daily, humble pursuit of people through sincere relationship.

This is tricky to discuss in broad and theoretical ways. The best way to engage this question is to engage people. Commit to loving people the way you would want to be loved in any given situation, and then commit to humility should they ask you to love them differently. Steadfast love and the choice to put humility over pride are two of the most Christlike things there are.

When we know all this, the question becomes: What are *your* boundaries while you pursue others? Often we won't need to challenge the boundaries of *others*. Rather, we will contend with our own "boundaries," by which I don't mean setting up fences that are healthy for us, but rather protecting our own comfort and avoiding difficult situations. In an interview with psychologists, journalist Helen Carefoot writes,

> Shrouding preferences in the therapy-speak language of boundaries is dangerous because it grants those preferences a certain amount of unwarranted credibility. And the resulting confusion (Are you fairly asking me to respect your boundaries, or are you trying to control me?) can contribute to hurt, says Dr. Manly. "It's tricky because we use the word boundary so loosely that all of us can slip into that and say, 'You crossed my boundary because you didn't do what I want you to do,' but that's just not how 'boundary' is used."[2]

When we commit to living with the kind of steadfast love that God shows us, we choose a countercultural path. One that might not make sense to a lot of people—even some Christians—and one that even fewer will actually walk. We shouldn't expect this love to be comfortable for us; we should expect pushback.

Remember what Jesus said to His disciples: "If the world hates you, keep in mind that it hated me first. If you belonged to the world, it would love you as its own. As it is, you do not belong to the world, but I have chosen you out of the world. That is why the world hates you" (John 15:18–19). People may resist your efforts to love them and may be baffled by your refusal to leave the way so many others have. *That's the sweet spot.*

That might mean some days feel thankless and some relationships remain a source of great hurt and frustration. You may feel taken advantage of by unhealthy people who treat you poorly because they know you are committed to caring for them. Most often, people may act completely indifferent to your efforts, making you wonder if any of this is worth it and tempting you to withdraw. It's exhausting to keep putting yourself out there when you might not ever see results (being married to a pastor, I can confirm this).

Although I know this may be tender territory, I want to ask you sincerely: Have you walked away from difficult relationships and challenging people because you were offended when they didn't respond to your kindness the way they should have? I have. Plenty of times. Even recently.

Fine, I'll give you an example. Not long ago, we moved into a new house in a new neighborhood. My husband and I had all these lovely conversations about wanting to be a blessing in our neighborhood and wanting to know our neighbors. I spent an afternoon putting together gifts for our neighbors, with homemade cookies and a heartfelt note with our information. We delivered them as a family, one by one, and I was *sure* that this act of outreach would result in myriad new friendships and deep, meaningful community. You'll be shocked to hear that it didn't. Sure, we have gotten to know some of our neighbors (and it has been lovely!), but just as many of them continue to pull into their garages and shut their doors without so much as a hello.

I have been tempted to say, "Well, I tried!" or "Their loss!" as an excuse to stop making an effort. Admittedly, I felt silly delivering Christmas gifts to the porches of neighbors who still haven't acknowledged us. Most people would say I have done my part. Looking at how our calendars are packed with work commitments and toddler activities and friendships with people who do want to get to know us, I am often tempted to give up on our vision for blessing our neighborhood. On occasion, I have justified my lack of perseverance and the walls I've built in my heart as ways of protecting my peace, as though they were healthy, necessary boundaries.

But I know God has blessed us to be a blessing for others in a real and tangible way. I know that we're not here by accident. I know that, when I really think about it, God will bless us with the energy and the strength to keep making the first move time after time. Because that's who He is.

God is love. God is *khesed* love that doesn't burn out or give up. God is love that genuinely wants to see others thrive, not just to assert itself. Ever since I said yes to following Jesus, that same love is part of my DNA. Christ followers are not people who give up on people when they offend us, or who wither and withdraw into themselves when our efforts aren't as valued as perhaps they should be. *Khesed* love isn't transactional; *khesed* love sticks around.

Remember that Jesus washed the feet of Judas Iscariot, knowing that hours later Judas would betray Him with a kiss and send Him into the hands of His accusers. He washed the feet of Peter, who denied Him three times in the moment of His greatest pain. He washed the feet of every disciple who later scattered when things got hard. After these betrayals, He went to the cross for their salvation, and the salvation of the Sanhedrin whom He offended, and the salvation of the Roman guards who held the hammer that nailed Him to the cross.

Was Jesus a doormat? Of course He wasn't. Jesus lived the single most powerful act in human history and bore the scars on His own body. He was God, and He decided that in humility, there would be ultimate power; that in death, life would burst forth. In Jesus, we see wholly empowered self-sacrifice. This is what He calls us to.

Ironically, the key to pursuing others in steadfast love is to embrace the power God has given you. I'm not talking about power in the worldly or cultural senses, in which that word often equates to total control or uninhibited choice. I'm talking about stepping into the powerful identity God has given you as His child: "Yet to all who did receive him, to those who believed in his name, he gave the right to become children of God—children born not of natural descent, nor of human decision or a husband's will, but born of God" (John 1:12–13).

When you truly know and believe your value as a child of the God of the universe, you find the self-worth needed to enforce necessary boundaries, as well as the ability to choose self-sacrifice the way Jesus did. Power dynamics are essential to keep in mind when you think about boundaries. If you paid attention to the Me Too movement, you may remember how many women shared stories of abuse at the hands of their male supervisors at work. Whether they felt pressure to laugh at jokes that crossed lines or were forced into unwanted sexual interactions, many women didn't speak up at first because the men in question held power over them. They endured an abuse of power because their coworkers could hurt their careers and threaten their livelihoods. When the player with more power crosses the boundary of the player with less power, that is inherently harmful.

Our God of justice hates exploitation and abuse. God calls for the protection of the "quartet of the vulnerable"[3]—orphans, widows, sojourners, and the poor (Zechariah 7:9–10)—because these four groups are especially vulnerable to exploitation and mistreatment. God's judgment of Israel stems from His people's failure to care for these groups. Indeed, this is one of the key indicators of Israel's pursuit of false gods over faithfulness to the true One.

> "Is not this the kind of fasting I have chosen:
> to loose the chains of injustice
>   and untie the cords of the yoke,
> to set the oppressed free
>   and break every yoke?
> Is it not to share your food with the hungry
>   and to provide the poor wanderer with shelter—

when you see the naked, to clothe them,
and not to turn away from your own flesh and blood?
Then your light will break forth like the dawn,
and your healing will quickly appear;
then your righteousness will go before you,
and the glory of the Lord will be your rear guard." (Isaiah 58:6–8)

Choosing self-sacrifice is vastly different from being *forced* to sacrifice yourself. Unequivocally, I am not calling you to endure abusive behavior at the hands of someone in your life, and I am not calling you to white-knuckle situations that cause you harm in the name of modeling God's pursuit of you. *Choosing* to risk the possibility that others might take advantage of you is an empowered Christlike choice. Friend, if someone is forcing you to acquiesce to *their* desires by calling for your deference, selflessness, humility, or steadfast love, that's exploitation and perhaps even abuse. I want to be crystal clear: Steadfast love that bears with difficult people is the result of an empowered God-given choice to do so, not the selfish manipulation of another human being.

Pursuing people who are difficult and continuing to show up for those who hurt our feelings requires that we are coming from a place of God-given empowerment and choosing to set ourselves aside for the sake of others. Should this become compulsory, imbalanced, harmful, or unbearably painful, I want you to return to square one: You are a child of God Most High, who values you so highly that He died so you might live.

I can't tell you which of *your* boundaries are there to protect your pride instead of your health, and I would never want to—that's a job for you and the Holy Spirit. A healthy boundary for me may be an excuse to withdraw for someone else, or vice versa. I am sure that God wants you to enforce and honor boundaries, both your own and others'. I also know that pursuing people often means detaching our commitment to love others from our satisfaction with their response. Mercifully, God calls all of us to the kind of community that models a covenant, and this community is a picture of how He has covenanted Himself to us:

> Therefore, as God's chosen people, holy and dearly loved, clothe yourselves with compassion, kindness, humility, gentleness and patience. Bear with each other and forgive one another if any of you has a grievance against someone. Forgive as the Lord forgave you. And over all these virtues put on love, which binds them all together in perfect unity. (Colossians 3:12–14)

Dig in here. In a world where we throw around terms like "boundaries," "protecting my peace," "toxic person," and the like, I want to gently step back and reset us toward the biblical picture of bearing *with*. Empowered self-sacrifice means we choose to forgive over and over, and we choose to bear with. Just because someone isn't responding to your kindness the way you want doesn't mean you need to cut them off because they're taking advantage of you. It doesn't mean they are toxic. They might just not be capable of receiving your love right now. Unrequited effort never once stopped Jesus from pursuing you, and He will strengthen us to keep showing up for people who reject us.

Empowered self-sacrifice also means refusing to let things break just because they're painful. Again, I am not talking about situations of abuse right now; I am talking about the natural and necessary pain of remaining in relationships with human beings who have different mindsets and backgrounds than yours. Plenty of healthy things hurt; that doesn't mean you should avoid them. Our temptation is to run from anything that causes discomfort (which I say with the qualifications of someone who hasn't exercised in about eighteen months). Sometimes this response is healthy! If your hand is on fire, you should probably deal with that ASAP before more damage is done to the rest of your body. If we live our lives afraid of pain and discomfort, though, we miss out on all the very best things.

My children are the funniest and most joyful people in my life right now. Today I woke up with a nineteen-month-old kissing my face. At lunch, my three-year-old said unprompted, "Mommy, you are my favorite girl!" Are you melting? I can hardly handle how much I love them.

But do you know what a combined forty hours of giving birth to my two children (thirty-six with the first, four with the second) felt like? Bad. It felt bad. Do you know how much I didn't want to wake up at 5:45 a.m. this morning when my daughter decided to be awake? That hurt too.

And I am so blessed by my marriage and by God allowing me to find my husband in college (my theory is that God knows I am altogether too weak to survive dating app culture). But growing up together from age twenty has been incredibly painful. The hurt we've worked through together has been nothing short of excruciating sometimes. Rarely are we both healthy and well-adjusted; at any given moment, one of us is carrying the other. The covenant of marriage is so beautiful and so painful at times.

In our pain, we are mercifully designed to produce thick, less sensitive flesh called *scar tissue* where wounds once were. God built us a system for pain management when we are wounded. Thus, like boundaries, scar tissue is healthy. But also like boundaries, when it sometimes grows unchecked and in places it shouldn't be, scar tissue ceases to offer any benefit and causes harm. *Fibrosis* is the medical term for when too much scar tissue forms, impeding function and resulting in additional pain. When scar tissue ceases to be restorative, it becomes a risk factor. We need the power of Jesus Christ to keep our hearts soft for others in our world of selfishness, and He faithfully provides this power. When we encounter the inevitable pain of loving people, let us run to Jesus to remind us of our identity and give us hearts of flesh (Ezekiel 36:26).

Despite the inherent pain found in many of life's most beautiful things, the beauty comes when we show up in the day-to-day even when it ceases to be fun. If we can't show up for the difficult and the painful, we will miss so much of the hard-won beauty. If we can have this same mentality when we bear with one another and embody wholly empowered self-sacrifice, we will find ourselves pursuing others the way God pursues us. In Philippians 2:5–8 we are exhorted to approach our relationships with the same mindset as Christ Jesus:

> Who, being in very nature God,
> did not consider equality with God something
> to be used to his own advantage;
> rather, he made himself nothing
> by taking the very nature of a servant,
> being made in human likeness.
> And being found in appearance as a man,
> he humbled himself
> by becoming obedient to death—
> even death on a cross!

Jesus had every reason not to suffer and not to live thirty-three years in the suffering that is humanity on earth, but He set aside comfort and authority for us. If Jesus, totally justified in His entitlement to those things, could do that, then surely we, with our vastly inflated sense of entitlement (especially in this day and age), can do the same to serve others. We can set healthy boundaries that bear with others in their suffering, even when they take it out on us or outright reject the love we offer them. In Christ, we don't let people walk out of our lives without a fight—not a fight against them, but a fight for their good and to bless them. As we partner with Christ for His redemption of all things, we forgive easily and carry heavy things with those who are suffering (Galatians 6:2–5). *We bear with.*

Pursuing people the way God pursues us most often looks like this: inviting people into your life and continuing to initiate and reach out, even when it's hard. A great place to start is by asking others for help; while I know this might be counterintuitive, you are setting the precedent that it's okay and good for them to subsequently invite you into *their* need. The beauty of this practice is that you also have to set aside your pride and adopt a posture of humility, instead of maintaining a false image of self-sufficiency. Asking for help is an underrated spiritual discipline, and it will open the door for you to meet others in their places of need. Give it a try.

Pursuing people the way God pursues us also means that ghosting is officially not in our day-to-day vocabulary. According to *Merriam-Webster*, the official definition of ghosting is "the act or practice of abruptly cutting off all contact with someone (such as a former romantic partner) usually without explanation by no longer accepting or responding to phone calls, instant messages, etc."[4] A less popular synonym for ghosting is just abandonment (but that is a decidedly less playful way of putting it). The point is: God doesn't just go dark on us, and we're not going to go dark on others. When relationships get hard, Jesus has modeled how to lean in and be present when others would leave, and He empowers us to do the same. If we have to leave a relationship, end a friendship, find a new church, etc., God has given us the maturity and soundness of mind to enter conflict and difficult conversations. He fights for our hearts every day, and He expects us to fight for the hearts of others before we walk out on them. Ghosting is not for followers of Jesus.

Finally, modeling God's pursuit of us looks like asking a lot of questions. Sometimes we get it in our heads that loving others in a Christlike manner has to look a particular way, such as writing notes with Bible verses or initiating frequent conversations about the Bible. These are both good things, most often meant sincerely. However, loving people—who are unique and individual as God has created us all—means we first must seek to know the hearts of the people we are trying to love. Being all-knowing, God has the benefit of already knowing exactly who we are and what we need. As humans, we are called to sincerely seek relationships with others to love them well; drive-by acts of love and service will never be as effective as the hard work of deeply knowing someone. The other benefit of this calling is that you don't have to be the authority driving the situation forward and holding all the answers. You get to show up with a holy, God-given love for another person, and you get to enter their story. Along the way, God stays close, showing you how to respond and what to say so you can reach this individual right where they are. God grows your compassion and your wisdom; God lets you see why her edges are so rough or why he shut down. God made us as individuals, and He wants us to approach one another as such. If you want to join God's pursuit of His people, learn the holiness of asking questions. Seek to know, more than you insist on being seen and known.

We are all boundary breachers. At the very beginning, God set boundaries for us that would render our health and flourishing, and we crossed them. Humans have set boundaries, crossed boundaries, and harmed one another ever since. To pursue people the way God pursues us, we must seek a redeemed understanding of healthy boundaries, both for ourselves and for others.

Ultimately, God's pursuit of us is to reel us back and reposition us within the boundary lines that will enable us to live abundantly. In this same spirit, we find the walls we've constructed to protect our pride, and we tear them down. We also make every effort to treat others with dignity, to be aware of their God-given uniqueness and autonomy, and to honor boundaries we may disagree with. As followers of Jesus bent on seeking the lost and bearing with the hurting, we choose the radical way of empowered self-sacrifice, one that enables us to fight for justice for others as we deny ourselves for the good of the other. Boundaries that help us bear with people mark the way we pursue others, even when people are difficult and it's uncomfortable.

The psalmist writes, "Lord, you alone are my portion and my cup; you make my lot secure. The boundary lines have fallen for me in pleasant places; surely I have a delightful inheritance" (Psalm 16:5–6). We can do this, friend. We can love better and truer and more deeply, and we can refuse to let our own pride and fickle feelings call the shots about how we do it. Pursue others, because He has pursued you.

CHAPTER 10

MUTUAL PURSUIT

Did anyone else grow up with parents who encouraged and enabled a princess obsession? Parents who bought you every Disney princess costume and made sure you had all the soundtracks memorized? Perhaps every birthday party from ages three to eight was pink and sparkly. Maybe on one particularly memorable occasion, your dad was forced to dress as Prince Charming to entertain a bunch of five-year-old girls (wait, that one is just me?). It's okay, you're safe here. Raise those hands. Own it. This is who you are.

Along with the movies and the costumes came the message that you were the most beautiful, most special, smartest, kindest girl in the world, and you should never let anyone treat you as anything other than that.

As you got older and entered the world of dating, this message stuck around: Any boy worth your time should treat you like the princess you are. Worthy princes scale towers and fight dragons for the object of their affection, and she just . . . waits (beautifully, of course).

This way of thinking has some substantial upsides, flawed though it may be. I went through middle school and high school with sky-high self-esteem and a strong aversion to being treated poorly or taken advantage of. When many of my friends were sprinting past their personal boundaries and values to win the affection of boys who barely seemed to care about them, I found myself completely repelled (if not offended) by boys who didn't seem to realize my value. Was I a bit entitled with a slight superiority complex? Sure. That's the dark side of the princess complex.

But I also only dated boys who genuinely cared about me and, at the time, seemed to think I hung the moon. I didn't believe I should have to chase after boys, so I simply *didn't*. The dating relationships I did have were the result of someone else putting in the effort to pursue me. With a couple of exceptions (since I was young and occasionally very, very dumb), I genuinely believe that I only dated good and kind young men. Looking at how it could have gone, I consider this to be a major advantage of princess culture.

Then I started dating the man I would marry. Even though I had been the first one to fall in love, he spent the five years of our dating relationship pursuing me with letters, gifts, and attentive affection. He flew out to Colorado days after our first date to meet my family and maintain the momentum of our new romance. He found a way to send me roses in Istanbul, Turkey, when I was studying abroad on our first Valentine's Day as a couple. He arranged the perfect proposal, popping the question while we were in a photo booth so every frame of my surprise and joy could be captured. He was so good at pursuing me.

When we finally started our life together, though, the princess complex posed a real problem. I had been accidentally conditioned to believe that true love meant being the beautiful main character and that the prince should be the one to do all the heavy lifting. I hadn't really put in much effort to respond to Tanner's pursuit, and before long, he was feeling burned out and unloved. To restore health and genuine romance in our marriage, I had to learn how to respond to my husband's pursuit of me . . . by pursuing *him*.

Pursuit shouldn't happen in a vacuum. While it might align with the princess and rom-com narratives that say you must be incessantly sought after (despite and *because* of your indifference), unrequited pursuit is not complete. For pursuit to achieve what it's meant to do, we must respond to it.

The same is true of God's pursuit. One purpose of this book is to convince you that God is pursuing you, always has pursued you, and always will pursue you—to make sure you know that He will not be dissuaded by your failure or your rejection. Unlike my husband (who, despite his many amazing qualities, is still a flawed human being), God doesn't require my validation or response to continue fighting for my heart. However, for God's pursuit to accomplish its purpose and bring its intended end, we must learn how to respond to it. God pursues us so that we can experience full, whole, healthy, and abundant life. Our hearts are designed for Him. Don't you want to live a life that realizes the beauty of being pursued by God and the joy of knowing that your Creator is always seeking your heart?

While it is true that God always initiates the pursuit, He calls us into active relationship with Him too. We are not pretty princesses sitting in the tower; we have been endowed with agency, the ability to say yes with our actions to the pursuit of the God of the universe. To live fully alive, we must learn to live in the light of God's pursuit. This journey takes place in three distinct ways: repair (through repentance), communication (through prayer), and adoration (also through prayer and through worship, which we will discuss further in the next chapter). We'll dive into each of these, but I'll tell you right now: Responding to God's efforts to enter a relationship with us does, in many important ways, resemble what we need to do to have a healthy relationship with *anyone*. I love that. As He does in so many areas of our lives, God has offered us a tangible, intuitive picture of how things in His kingdom operate. Maintaining healthy, thriving relationships with other humans points to the same practices that will help us grow a healthy, thriving relationship with Him. *No matter what, passivity isn't an option.* Not if you want true life to the full (John 10:10). You have to participate.

First is repentance. Let's begin in Romans 2, verses 4 and 8: "God's kindness is intended to lead you to repentance. . . . But for those who are self-seeking and who reject the truth and follow evil, there will be wrath and anger." Jesus comes after you, no matter where you are, to rescue you from sin and death.

Sometimes that sin comes from bad choices or shortsighted mistakes. Sometimes sin in your life is the result (whether direct or indirect) of darkness you were thrown into by no choice of your own. But He is merciful. He is kind. He is relentless.

The purpose of God's kindness, per Romans, is not just to leave you feeling warm and fuzzy, but to lead you to repentance. So what is repentance? Anytime you look at your life patterns and say, "This isn't good, and this isn't working," you are mere steps away from a drastic change in your heart. In those moments, Jesus is right there with you, waiting for you to surrender your ways in favor of His. I know *repentance* seems like a religious word closely associated with fire and brimstone and legalism, but repentance is ultimately the confession that your attempts to engineer abundance on your own won't work—it is a confession that you need God. God takes repentance so seriously because any sin we allow to exist in our life reveals some part of our heart that we don't want Him to have.

We use the word *sin* so much and in such a narrow context (i.e., "bad things" that good Christians shouldn't do) that we actually don't know what it means. In the Bible, the Hebrew word *khata* and the Greek word *hamartia* both have the same translation: to fail, to miss a goal.[1] This isn't about doing something bad so much as failing to live up to something better. God's intention and design for everything is perfect and full. Anytime we take matters into our own hands with the intention of doing things our own way or achieving some fictional higher good than God's good, we will inevitably miss our goal. Our designs and plans will fail—they have to. We can't possibly succeed outside the designs and plans of our Creator. Thus, sin is far less about violating some arbitrary boundary set by a stoic, distant God (as I fear many of us think), and far more about a false conception of reality. Either we believe something wrong about ourselves and are under the immature illusion that we have what it takes to create the reality we want, or we believe something wrong about God and are unaware of His perfect wisdom and His deep, merciful love for us. Ultimately, we don't believe that God loves us so much that He built beautiful, glorious things into His plan for us to experience if only we would follow.

Repentance, then, is to surrender to a reality we may not fully understand, and to submit to a King we know to be good. We realign ourselves with truth, which allows God to use us and allows us to live in union with God.

When I was in high school, I went through a season when I felt like God was far from me. Hearing God speak, mostly through the Bible and prayer, usually came easy for me. During this season, my prayers felt hollow and the Bible felt dull. One night, in a state of anxious half-sleep, I felt led to open my Bible to Hebrews 3:

> See to it, brothers and sisters, that none of you has a sinful, unbelieving heart that turns away from the living God. But encourage one another daily, as long as it is called "Today," so that none of you may be hardened by sin's deceitfulness. We have come to share in Christ, if indeed we hold our original conviction firmly to the very end. As has just been said:

> "Today, if you hear his voice,
> do not harden your hearts
> as you did in the rebellion."
>
> (Hebrews 3:12–15, quoting Psalm 95:7–8)

The author of Hebrews continues, explaining how hearts hardened by sin ultimately kept the Israelites from entering God's rest. When I read this passage in high school, the Holy Spirit convicted me of sin patterns, behaviors, and habits I had embraced in my life and knew were wrong. I was having fun, and I had found a way to justify my disobedience to the Lord. "I'm young! This is so normal! I will be a better Christian when I'm older! All my mentors made these same mistakes!" On and on. I convinced myself I could withhold that specific area of my life from God but still grow deeper in my faith in all the spaces where I would allow Him in.

God woke me up and said: There is no rest apart from surrender to the voice of God. If He has spoken, either through Scripture or through the Holy Spirit's prompting, we will only experience rest once we listen to His words. When we choose to create a comfortable space for sin in our lives, we then also must find a way to drown out the voice of God. Essentially, if you want to keep sinning while also remaining a follower of Jesus, you will end up building a wall between you and Him. Repentance gives God the go-ahead to tear down that wall and restore the connection and closeness you ran from to appease your sin.

Although that sleepless night with Hebrews 3 was pivotal in my understanding of how sin operates, I sometimes catch myself drifting back into that weird spiritual compartmentalization.

Can you relate? We give God *almost* everything, but our hearts hang on to certain dreams, relationships, habits, or vices. We have the underlying belief that we will be happier if we are allowed to be our own god.

In Hosea 6 we see a picture of false repentance. This kind of repentance wants healing and restoration, but on its own terms. This kind of religion checks all the right boxes and looks pious on the outside, but it is full of pride at its core.

> "Come, let us return to the LORD.
> He has torn us to pieces
>   but he will heal us;
> he has injured us
>   but he will bind up our wounds.
> After two days he will revive us;
>   on the third day he will restore us,
>   that we may live in his presence.
> Let us acknowledge the LORD;
>   let us press on to acknowledge him.
> As surely as the sun rises,
>   he will appear;
> he will come to us like the winter rains,
>   like the spring rains that water the earth."
>
> "What can I do with you, Ephraim?
>   What can I do with you, Judah?
> Your love is like the morning mist,
>   like the early dew that disappears.

Therefore I cut you in pieces with my prophets,
I killed you with the words of my mouth—
then my judgments go forth like the sun.
For I desire mercy, not sacrifice,
and acknowledgment of God rather than
burnt offerings." (Hosea 6:1–6)

Israel acknowledges that God has the power to heal. The Israelites return to God with their lips, but their hearts remain distant. Throughout Hosea 6 and 7, we see this call to repentance juxtaposed with declarations of Israel's unfaithfulness to God. They don't want God; they want God's benefits.

We all know this song and dance. "God, I'll go back to church if You fix *x* situation." "I promise I will stop sinning if You let me have *y* opportunity." Israel knew this routine too. All too well. They turn back to God, but only to escape the consequences of their behavior, which we clearly see in Hosea, throughout the book of Judges, and even in the Psalms of David. They return to the checklist of things they know they are supposed to do as God's people, and God sees right through it. Lip service seems like a solution, yet it only brings further confusion and exhaustion. Finding true rest requires true repentance, which requires the submission of our entire lives in turn. We lay down sin so we can finally lie down. We pick up a cross that demands everything yet paradoxically offers an easy yoke (Matthew 11:30).

The Lion of Judah tore the Israelites away from their idols, and it hurt. If I allow my idols deep enough in my heart, getting ripped from their clutches seems to threaten my life itself. The words of God's prophets felt like violence when the Israelites' identity was their rebellion. God's word became a weapon because it had to kill the death they had permitted to live within them. God knew that the Israelites, just like us, didn't necessarily want Him as much as they just wanted to feel better.

True repentance comes when our lives and our hearts mirror God's own. Internal change (such as what is demonstrated by welcoming mercy) will always beat the external show of religion (which may be represented by offering sacrifices). For our external demonstrations of our dedication to God to truly matter, we first must truly repent.

Theologian Sam Storms writes, "Refusal to repent is to elevate our own souls above God's glory, but when one does repent, it leads to the forgiveness of sin, the removal of divine discipline, and the restoration of one's experiential communion with God."[2] When God pursues us, the first way we respond to His pursuit is to repent and let Him tear down that final wall separating us from all He is trying to give us.

If repentance is our admission that we're lost, prayer is how we turn toward God and pursue *Him*. In prayer, we find relational intimacy with God. I have often envied the people who instantly beam when they talk about their relationship with the Lord, smiling as if they so clearly feel His love and delight for them. When I started to take prayer seriously, I found that the key to moving through the world assured of God's delight is to regularly communicate with Him. Would you expect your relationship with a new friend or a romantic interest to grow without conversation? Of course not. So it is with prayer.

According to Dallas Willard,

> The most adequate description of prayer is simply, "Talking to God about what we are doing together." That immediately focuses the activity where we are but at the same time drives the egotism out of it. Requests will naturally be made in the course of this conversational walk. Prayer is a matter of explicitly sharing with God my concerns about what he too is concerned about in my life. And of course he is concerned about my concerns and, in particular, that my concerns should coincide with His. This is our walk together. Out of it I pray.[3]

Prayer is an ongoing conversation with the One whom we want to know more. At its core, prayer is just communication, from us to God and from God to us. We acknowledge His closeness, and we reach out for more. I don't believe we *can* experience God's supernatural power at its fullest apart from prayer. The people of Israel saw God's might when He sent them into exile, but no one wants to be on the disciplinary end of God's wrath. For us to experience the glorious and abundant beauty of life with God, the closeness and trust that develop from and propel us into prayer are key.

In seasons when God feels far off, I have wondered, *Where are You, Lord? Why aren't You showing up?* But think about it: God might be meeting a million different needs a day, and we wouldn't see this as the intentional care and provision that it is if we never vocalized our needs to God in the first place. In that sense, prayer is for *us*. We get to vulnerably share our needs with God, and then we get the thrill of watching Him respond. Our faith in His goodness grows, and our trust that He hears us grows along with it. If we don't give God an opportunity to show His generosity, we will always think He is tightfisted.

For those of us who are particularly prone to wander, prayer is how we see God's grace in daily action *without* us rebelling, reaching rock bottom, and crying out in a last-ditch moment of desperation. For that reason (and because we are all prone to wander), prayer is essential: We need regular reminders of God's goodness to keep us close to Him, and we need to avoid the inevitable damage we do to ourselves and to others when we start to run away.

Have you ever found yourself feeling guilty for prayers that feel like long lists of "God, please do this" and "Lord, please do that"? I have. Almost always, actually. I've heard sermon after sermon about so-called Christians who don't truly want God, just what God can give them. I don't want to be a "moralistic therapeutic deist," which is the term sociologists Christian Smith and Melinda Lundquist Denton use to describe the general religious attitude of young people.[4] They're moralistic because they think God wants them to be good people; therapeutic because their spiritual practices focus mostly on making themselves feel better about their lives; and deist because they vaguely believe in a higher power who remains detached and mostly uninvolved. A colloquial way of putting it: God is my vending machine.

After my miscarriage, in my hopelessness and anxiety, I read Psalm 131:

> My heart is not proud, LORD,
> my eyes are not haughty;
> I do not concern myself with great matters
> or things too wonderful for me.
> But I have calmed and quieted myself,
> I am like a weaned child with its mother;
> like a weaned child I am content.
>
> Israel, put your hope in the LORD
> both now and forevermore.

At the time, this passage felt like God's gentle invitation for me to stop begging for answers and trying to Google what was wrong with me. It was precisely that. God wanted me to cuddle up and understand that being close to Him was enough.

Since then, I have fed and weaned my own children. I'm currently nursing one of my kids (Thea), and the other (Judah) has been fully weaned for nearly two years. The difference between them is when I pull Thea into my lap, she instantly tries to nurse. "Milk! Milk!" she yells at me (totally unrelated sidenote: I think it's time to wean). It's not sinful, and it's not her fault. It's a force of habit and she is still a baby. Judah, on the other hand, just loves to be close to me. He will snuggle, lay his head on my chest, and rest there.

But let me assure you: Judah, my weaned child content in my arms, still asks me for things, like, 150 times a day. "Mama, I'm thirsty for water!" "Mama, may you please get me some apples?" "Mama, I got a big ow. Can you kiss it?" I hear about Judah's needs constantly, because even though he is weaned, he is still a toddler who needs me.

Psalm 131 isn't about vilifying our needs or somehow loving God's presence so much that we no longer have any needs. The psalmist surely *could* have written, "Like a fully self-sufficient friend wholly different and apart from You, I am content." But he didn't. Because weaned children are not independent or self-sufficient. They long for closeness and find contentment in being held by their mother, and they remain profoundly dependent on her too. Whereas nursing infants are mostly just aware of their primal need for nourishment and warmth, weaned children have reached the developmental point where relational closeness also meets a need. It's not an either-or; it's a both-and.

When we, like my son Judah, realize that closeness to our provider is just as much a need as our need for food, we find the sweet spot of prayer. Within prayer, both our physical and relational needs are met. As David says in Psalm 63:1 (ESV), our need for God's presence eventually becomes as urgent as our physical needs:

> O God, you are my God; earnestly I seek you;
>   my soul thirsts for you;
> my flesh faints for you,
>   as in a dry and weary land where there is no water.

Prayer is how we pursue God back. Prayer is how we respond to the realization that God draws near. But we're not God. This isn't about a mutual pursuit in which we're out to match God's effort. We're not on the same level of power or sovereignty; God doesn't need us to meet His needs. Our pursuit is driven largely by our need for Him, which includes closeness with Him as well as provision for our day-to-day needs.

And guess what? God is okay with that. God *loves* that. God designed us with needs and weaknesses. He doesn't expect you to become so strong and independent that you don't need Him to provide and that you can enter this relationship as an equal party. He designed you to have needs, and He specifically intended that you come to Him to meet those needs. You are like a weaned child who knows that God delights to feed and protect you, and His strong, tender arms are the most peaceful place you can nestle into.

If you're struggling to believe that God wants your list of needs and wants you to jump into His lap like a sweet and needful three-year-old, read Psalm 103:

> Praise the Lord, my soul,
> and forget not all his benefits—
> who forgives all your sins
> and heals all your diseases,
> who redeems your life from the pit
> and crowns you with love and compassion,
> who satisfies your desires with good things
> so that your youth is renewed like the
> eagle's. . . .

As a father has compassion on his children,
so the Lord has compassion on those who fear him;
for he knows how we are formed,
he remembers that we are dust.
(verses 2–5, 13–14)

Prayer is an act of God, something we need the Holy Spirit to empower us to do. Romans 8:14–17 says that the Holy Spirit gives us the ability to cry out to God by making us His children. The Spirit of God thus intercedes for us when we don't know what or how to pray. The moment God makes you His own, He initiates a conversation with you through His Spirit and invites you into His presence. How much we say yes to that conversation—to prayer—is how much we will fully realize our identity as kids of a good and powerful King.

From the beginning of time and throughout the whole world, God has pursued you. He is waiting for you to respond in repentance, in worship, and in prayer. Paul explains it to the Athenians like this:

> "The God who made the world and everything in it is the Lord of heaven and earth and does not live in temples built by human hands. And he is not served by human hands, as if he needed anything. Rather, he himself gives everyone life and breath and everything else. From one man he made all the nations, that they should inhabit the whole earth; and he marked out their appointed times in history and the

> boundaries of their lands. God did this so that they would seek him and perhaps reach out for him and find him, though he is not far from any one of us. 'For in him we live and move and have our being.' As some of your own poets have said, 'We are his offspring.'" (Acts 17:24–28)

He did all this—forming human beings, founding vibrant cultures, planning each act of history—so that you would reach out, perhaps in an act of desperation as you fumble through the darkness, to find out that He's been right here this whole time. In Him you live, move, and have your being; God will never stop drawing near. While God journeyed through galaxies and descended into the deepest darkness to pursue you, our reciprocal pursuit is really nothing more than an outstretched hand. But this small movement toward Him, this tiniest cry of surrender, is enough to unlock the kind of closeness with God you've wanted all your life. Our feeble human pursuit is just reaching out our arms as we fumble in the dark after the power has gone out. But this act of reaching out says something, doesn't it? It says we are lost and we know it. God is so merciful, both by allowing us the free will to choose and by making Himself so available.

You're not the powerless and entitled princess in the tower. You're not the main character of the story, and truthfully, you wouldn't want to be. Because of this God who pursues, you get to enter a story so much better than any Disney lore. You get to be the beloved child of a powerful and good King who values your every need and loves to hold you close. God doesn't need you to swim across oceans and climb over peaks. He knows you can't. God just wants your hand reaching out to Him and your eyes looking for something sturdy to cling to. Stretch out your arm and see how near He is.

CHAPTER 11

REVIVAL FROM REST

In addition to repentance and prayer, there is one more key piece of how we respond to God's pursuit of us: rest.

I recently went to a large conference for young millennial and Gen Z women. The worship was amazing, the speakers memorable, and the atmosphere contagious. Throughout the weekend, the leader of the conference voiced her sincere belief that this younger generation is ripe for revival. According to her, Generation Z has been plagued by anxiety and depression and hit hard by global calamities (like the pandemic), but with their generational boldness and desire to experience the supernatural, Gen Zers are being baptized in droves across college campuses.

I believe it. As a young millennial, I remember the days when the greatest threat to the faith of young people was atheism. Older Christians drilled us in apologetics, equipping us with information for the next time a skeptic put us on the spot. Knowing the logical basis for my faith certainly has been helpful, but I was led to believe that mean atheists would be a much bigger part of my day-to-day.

Talking to college students and young adults over the past few years, as well as developing a keen eye for internet trends, I can confidently report that interest in and openness to spiritual things continue to grow. Springtide Research Institute, an organization dedicated to gathering information about people between the ages of thirteen and twenty-five, found the following in a 2021 study: "More than half of young people say they never or rarely attend a religious service, but they do report engaging at least weekly in a few activities they consider religious or spiritual practices, including engaging in or with art (53%), praying (45%), reading (45%), or being in nature (40%)."[1] Their findings also suggest that Gen Zers are aware of how spirituality benefits their mental health, something they desperately need as the first generation to grow up with the internet and social media, on top of being impressionable adolescents during a pandemic.

We want revival. We *need* revival. This generation is hungry for the things of God, even if they may not know exactly where to look for Him. Young people today know that they're burned out and depressed, and the constant cast of blue light from a barrage of screens takes far more than it gives. They know that they're lonely and struggling to find community. They know that there is *more*, but they are not sure where to find it. Yet have we taken the time to break down the meaning of *revival* in the first place?

To revive is:

1. *to restore to consciousness or life*
2. *to restore from a depressed, inactive, or unused state: bring back*
3. *to renew in the mind or memory*[2]

Restore, renew, revive. These words all speak to a desire to bring something back and to see strength return and energy explode. Referencing William B. Sprague, Tim Keller defines *revival* in a narrower spiritual sense as "the intensification of the ordinary operations of the Holy Spirit," occurring mainly through the "ordinary, 'instituted means of grace'—preaching, pastoring, worship, prayer."[3] Even through those means, the power source is the Spirit, and the mechanism is simply His grace. Yet I can't help but notice that we keep calling for this revival in packed rooms and church services, in city squares and youth camps. We yell, plead, and call people out of their seats and into the baptismal. We harp on what we need to do in the world to bring Jesus back to it. In this collective of the exhausted, we unintentionally demand more action without realizing the cost.

When was the last time you pulled an all-nighter and then felt fully equipped to charge into a big work event? Or the last time you tossed and turned for hours, only to spring out of bed ready and able to love and serve your family well? Have you ever had one of those days when everything seemed to go wrong and you were depleted and sore? I'm guessing you didn't feel like yelling the good news from the rooftops. When we're physically and emotionally tired, showing up in our world becomes a lot harder. When we're exhausted, we struggle to truly experience God's abundance.

Will we ever stop to realize that, just maybe, our revivals will be fleeting and temporary if we cannot invite these tired masses into the *rest* that sustains vibrant life? Worship is indeed designed to draw us into this rest, but rest (as well as worship) encompasses more than just physical relaxation. God intentionally designed our bodies to embody spiritual realities. Can we recognize that, just like physical restoration requires a good night's sleep, spiritual revival requires true, full, and sustained patterns of rest?

I know the first step. To truly find our souls at rest, we must grasp the truth that Jesus Christ has drawn near to us and pursued us to whatever end. The God of the universe wants to set us free from strife and the endless cycles of sin, guilt, self-righteousness, and swearing we've changed until the next time we stumble. God invites us to a life of resting from the burdens of sin, scarcity, and control. When we finally realize that we are free to rest, we will find the revival we so desperately need.

Understanding God's pursuit gives us a place to lie down and a green pasture beside still waters so we can find true restoration. Knowing that the Creator and Sustainer of all things is in your corner imparts a profound sense of safety. We gain the freedom to move through life as people unshackled and aware that we really have nothing to lose.

Did you ever go on a ropes course? Maybe you were at camp and your cabin had its day on the big ropes course. You got your harness and your helmet on, found a partner, and started climbing. At the camp I went to growing up, the ropes course crisscrossed over the ground from forty feet above. With my harness on, I was fearless. I walked tightropes without faltering. I jumped from rope to rope without hesitation. By contrast, at least one girl in the group each summer was terrified to move. This girl took three hours to complete the course, largely because of the ten-minute pep talk she required at the start of each section. No amount of reassurance or explanation convinced her that the harness was secure and that the ropes and carabiners could hold her weight. (However, we were proud of her for trying at all!)

The difference between my jumping and leaping and laughing high in the treetops and her terror wasn't that I had stronger ropes or a better harness. The difference was that I believed I was totally safe, and she didn't.

A sense of safety affects your ability to rest. When I was twenty-two, I traveled around Europe with my friend Angela, another twenty-two-year-old woman. We tried to book Airbnb accommodations in safe neighborhoods, but our research abilities were limited by our lack of experience and lack of familiarity with these cities. In Budapest, our apartment (in a beautiful baroque building with large windows and high ceilings) had an old rickety doorknob and thin walls. At night, the single-pane antique windows let in all the light from the outside courtyard, and the thin curtains did very little other than projecting the shadows of passing figures. During one point in the night, I could have sworn I saw a dark figure linger by our doorway, and my heart skipped a beat when I heard quiet metallic scraping noises that sounded a lot like someone trying to pick the lock. Nothing ever happened that night (thankfully), including my sleeping a wink (less thankfully). I didn't feel safe, so I couldn't enter real rest.

Knowing that you are safe makes all the difference. You can enjoy the kind of rest that truly revives. Because we know we are safe and have a God who won't let us go, we can *find rest in the risk of following Jesus*. Because we know that Jesus will come after us wherever we may go, we can rest in the assurance that we are safe. Truly grasping God's pursuit and resting with that knowledge are key to lasting revival in the body of Christ.

As far as I can tell, we find ourselves exhausted by three primary things: sin, scarcity, and control. I know I've struggled with all three at different times (and sometimes more than one at the same time). Jesus, in His pursuit of us and by His drawing near, desires that we would be free from all three.

SIN

We've already discussed the importance of turning from our sin through repentance, but I want to touch on why sin is so profoundly exhausting. As I write this, I'm looking out the window of a coffee shop at a young woman (probably in her twenties) standing on the corner. She's been talking to everyone who comes her way, and strangers have mostly hurried by her without much more than an awkward headshake. I don't know exactly what she's saying, but I can make some guesses. A couple minutes ago, a man on a bike rode by, stopped, and pulled out a half-drunk bottle of what appeared to be Gatorade. They exchanged a few words, and then I watched her pull a twenty-dollar bill out of her bag, look around furtively, and slip it into his hand. I don't know what was in the bottle, but I do know that she chugged half of it within thirty seconds and started pacing the street and talking to herself, her movements jerky and unpredictable.

I understand that addiction is a complicated thing; I am not drawing a parallel from this situation to all sin. However, looking at this woman, I can see how absolutely exhausted she is. She is hunched over and squinting into the sun. She paces back and forth, across the intersection, and around the corner. Pacing, pacing, pacing. I want to help her find a place to just sit down and rest a little from a life that (from where I sit) looks like it must be really hard today. In the ninety-degree heat, she needs water and shade. This is our problem too, isn't it? Running to sources that can't heal or fill us in hopes of finding true sustenance only depletes us. The same is true of sin. We run ourselves ragged as we pace, going from one dopamine high to the next and hoping that *this time* we will find transcendence and purpose. But we won't. We will just be running forever. And running is the opposite of rest.

Within all of us, there is a constant war between the image of God and those fateful words that the serpent spoke to Eve in Genesis 3: "Did God really say that?" The Enemy doesn't want you at peace or whole; the Enemy doesn't want anything that resembles God to walk the face of this earth. Just as the serpent spoke to Eve, there will always be a little voice tempting you to try anything but God's way so you can attempt to maintain total power and autonomy.

Of course, total power and autonomy can't coexist with dependence on God or healthy relationships with others. Underneath sin is a thinly masked agenda to alienate us from the people who love us and the God who loves us even more. Sin is just endless striving in the dark. There's legalism, which demands our total perfection as a means of accessing God's favor. We know that's not right, since our salvation depends on Christ, not on us. Going the other direction—hurling ourselves headlong into evil—doesn't solve the constant struggle to be enough. Rather, sin positions us to strive to be enough for *ourselves*. We take the reins and do whatever feels good and right, asserting our free will and agency against God's. And where do we find ourselves? Healed, whole, and happy? No!

Doing whatever feels good is just as oppressive as trying to be perfect. Let me tell you what this looked like for me in a particularly dark season. One day, it felt good to ignore my best friend and her problems instead of sitting with her in her struggles. The next day, it felt good to do six tequila shots and be "crazy!" out with my friends, saying things I didn't mean with people I shouldn't have trusted and losing sleep I desperately needed. On another day, it felt good to go to the gym, but while I was there, I realized it would feel even better to have the ever-elusive perfect body. I was stuck trying to satisfy a long line of urges, many directly opposing one another. The heavy drinking and the perfect abs and the healthy relationships were all in tension. Have you also lived through a season like this? Maybe you were calling the shots, and that was cool (at least initially). But the result was merely a constant game of guilt and hiding, one that you will never win because the desires are at war within you (James 4:1). You can denounce the shame, but that doesn't mean it's not there. Human beings will *always* find a way to feel shame. To embrace sin is to embrace restlessness and partner with exhaustion.

We've already taken a deep dive into how we tackle sin through repentance. There's truly no other way. When sin depletes every good thing in you, you really have just two options: Either you surrender the sin before it levels you and trust that God's wisdom is better than your own, or you hit rock bottom. You destroy your relationships, you wreak havoc on your body, and you feel emptier than before, because not only are you now unhappy, but you've run into the painful reality that you don't even know how to help yourself. Most human beings can't learn how right God is without first learning how wrong they are; thus, most of us end up flat on our faces, too tired to stand up, and desperate for the miracle of God's help.

SCARCITY

Then there's scarcity. Sin and scarcity travel closely together. I can attest. A scarcity mindset convinces us that there is never enough, whether that's money, time, opportunity, power, love, attention, and so on. Friend, clutching anything other than Jesus is the definition of idolatry. It doesn't have to come by intentional rebellion or prideful bids for power; it might just be the result of the highly erroneous belief deep down that God messed up and didn't give you what He owed you. This belief is often about money, and the fear of being unable to provide for yourself and your family is enough to make you put your trust in a job or a bank account. Anyone who has ever been poor and then rich will tell you: Wealth didn't fix anything at all. It just meant the needs multiplied. Scarcity mentality—believing there isn't enough—rarely revolves around the need itself; it starts with fear (which is perhaps even valid), but it bleeds into your veins until nothing feels enough *ever.*

Maybe you don't feel pretty enough, and maybe you have a collection of memories from the time you were little to confirm it's true. If you let that lie take root, unmitigated by the biblical truth that you were made good and beautiful by a perfect God who *likes* you, you will spend the rest of your days envying people who do seem to possess that beauty. Resentment will start to grow too. Your money will never be enough to heal the deep wound of deficiency in you. No compliment, no human love, and no skincare routine will ever be able to change your mind. No matter what it applies to, a scarcity mentality will run you ragged, and it will always be closely followed by the real and significant threat of worshiping a false god.

Fighting against scarcity requires a staunch and almost irresponsible trust in God's provision. We must resist the urge to hustle, compete, or obsess over shortcomings and those places where we hear whispers (perhaps screams) of "not enough." Rest, then, is radical trust that God constantly runs after us with His goodness and mercy, and He will continue to do so when we stop trying so hard. It's the belief that God has already provided enough, because He loves us that deeply.

We return to the idea of God's pursuit coming through His provision. He will not falter in His power to give us what we need so that we can rest (as we must). When God sent manna to the Israelites in the desert in Exodus 16, He sent enough for each day, no more and no less. The day before the Sabbath, God sent double the amount of food. Then (and only on this specific day) the manna lasted for more than one day. This practice was intended to release the Israelites into a full dedicated day of rest. We embrace God's enoughness over our own (faltering as ours is), and we find ourselves abundantly full. God's pursuit through His provision frees us to enter the rest He commands for our good.

CONTROL

Control, although equally enticing and exhausting as sin and scarcity, masquerades as a kind of noble morality. It looks like conscientiousness or wisdom. You're constantly thinking ahead and planning your next move to ensure that nothing gets by you. Control is particularly addictive because it often works like a charm; when you micromanage each detail of your life with meticulous precision, you will very likely end up with a life that looks the way you want it to. But that's really the problem, isn't it? Control isn't a surrender to God's plan; it's a hostile takeover of His intention for you and your gifts. It's insisting on the comfort of your own trajectory because the risk of letting go feels too high.

You can't maintain control and rest at the same time, though. An estimated 17 percent of fatal car accidents from 2017 to 2021 involved at least one drowsy driver[4]—you can't maintain control of a vehicle and rest at the same time. Control and rest are a lethal combination because it simply can't work. I see control killing us spiritually and mentally too. Staying in the driver's seat 24-7 requires you to constantly look ahead, anticipating problems and agonizing over things that could go wrong. If you're not obsessing over the future, then you're obsessing over the past, especially the mistakes you've made, how you should have avoided them, and how they're holding you back now. Rarely, if ever, are control freaks like us just *present*.

But Jesus, God in the flesh, the Alpha and the Omega, spent His days on earth with people. Jesus didn't posture for power or influence, nor did He waste a single breath on what He "should" have done. For Christ, the perfect life looked like a calm commitment to being with the people He was with, in the places where His feet were standing. If Jesus is that Good Shepherd who can be trusted to guide you, His precious sheep, to green pastures, don't you think He wants you to have this perfect life too? His route and His pace are sure and true, so you can find rest from your constant attempts to control your life. You, too, can find peace in this present moment and in doing whatever God has set before you in the here and now. In Christ, and only in Christ, will you find the purpose your hungry heart is after.

No matter what is exhausting you, revival will come only when you lay it down and finally experience true rest. A cognitive process alone won't get the job done. You might be convinced by everything you just read that says you need rest, and you may even want it. But for you to be really revived and changed, though, the missing piece of the puzzle is worship. We are first brought to our knees by our exhaustion after striving, and then we are laid flat on our faces by God's mercy. The beautiful, gracious truth is that no matter why we lie down before Him, He grants rest to our bodies as we live out our gratefulness and awe. In rest is worship; in worship is rest.

> Shout for joy to the Lord, all the earth.
> Worship the Lord with gladness;
> come before him with joyful songs.
> *Know that the Lord is God.*
> *It is he who made us, and we are his;*
> *we are his people, the sheep of his pasture.*
> (Psalm 100:1–3, emphasis added)

For the psalmist, this acknowledgment of who God is flows directly into praise. Through worshiping the Lord with gladness, we live in our bodies what we know to be true about who made us and whom we belong to. Worship is profoundly theological; it is the proclamation of who God is as expressed by our nervous system, our muscles, and our very cells. Worship is both declaration and formation; as we continue to testify about God's character in our worship, the Holy Spirit continues His work in our hearts.

In *You Are What You Love: The Spiritual Power of Habit*, author James K. A. Smith writes,

> Worship works from the top down, you might say. In worship we don't just come to show God our devotion and give him our praise; we are called to worship because in this encounter God (re)makes and molds us top-down. Worship is the arena in which God recalibrates our hearts, reforms our desires, and rehabituates our loves. Worship isn't just something we do; it is where God does something to us. Worship is the heart of discipleship because it is the gymnasium in which God retrains our hearts.[5]

To worship is to align your heart, soul, mind, and strength—all of you—with truth. It's celebrating a victory you know to be true, even as you wait for its full realization in the here and now.

As a response to God's pursuit, worship is thus the truest way to tell God, "I don't want to run anymore. I want all of me near all of You. I know Your goodness and mercy have followed me all this time, and I want to experience them in their fullness for once."

Like the disingenuous Israelites, whose repentance was all in their heads and meant to accomplish a certain end, we've all had those moments when we promise God we'll stop sinning and be better (whatever that means!). I've been at enough youth camps to have heard "I want to get closer to God" more times than I can count. The problem is that camp ends and we go home. I imagine you've had a "mountaintop experience" with God; you went to a retreat, conference, camp, or even a place where you could just be alone with God for a few hours, and you encountered God's goodness there. In that moment, you felt so energized and motivated to change your life and finally be the person God made you to be. You probably wrote a long journal entry declaring the changes ahead. Maybe you told a friend. You likely cried. But when you returned to your normal environment and struggles, the same sin patterns were still there. You got a small taste of what your life could look like, and you loved it, but your real life still had all the complications and challenges that set the stage for your running away in the first place.

Don't read these words and think I'm writing off these powerful moments with God, because I am absolutely not. I believe these moments of repentance—the realignment of your life with God's truth—are sincere and true. I think they are proof of how God pursues each of us individually and ardently. These moments often occur in the middle of a big decision or big need, and the Lord has often initiated the process of my repentance by directing me, providing for me, or healing me.

The problem is that we don't often let these mountaintop moments of repentance sink into the depths of our hearts and the marrow of our bones. The thrill of hearing the gospel, for the first time or once again, surely excites our minds and our spirits. But the only way to truly fuse the gospel with our bodies is through worship.

Think about your physical fitness for a moment. Weight lifting is having a moment right now; we know that resistance training offers significant benefits to our overall health.[6] It makes sense: The more we put our muscles through controlled stress, the better our muscles can sustain stress when it's not controlled. We seek discomfort with the goals of endurance and health. In weight training, our muscles release hormones that benefit our mental health, as well as other systems in the body. If you've ever experienced the endorphins of an insanely hard workout, you know what I'm talking about—there's almost nothing like it. Sidenote: If weight training isn't a part of your life, start now!

When we lift heavy weights, we intentionally tear our muscle fibers and trigger our bodies to repair those muscle fibers. In the process, they're made stronger. Our souls strengthen the same way; repentance is the intentional act of discomfort that we choose, and we trust that the purported benefits are real. When we repent, we often experience a spiritual high. But we can't stop there.

To get the most out of exercise, we also must give our bodies time to recover. The repair process that our bodies initiate to strengthen our muscles over time? It can't happen if we don't stop. To fully realize the benefits of physical exercise, we have to balance the exertion with rest.

Alternatively, consider how the human brain stores its memories. We can cram as much information as we want into our brains, but if we don't rest, our brains won't be able to encode that information into true learning. As a high school and college student, I was a chronic crammer—unlike some of my more responsible friends, I cannot remember ever studying for an exam more than a day or two ahead, and I regularly pulled all-nighters to do so. At the time, my parents and teachers insisted,

"Cramming doesn't work!" And I was certain they were lying because . . . it did work. I continued to get good marks using this method. Now, several years after my formal academic studies, I can confirm: *Cramming absolutely does not work.* I remember general concepts from school, but facts and references? Zero. Nothing. Blank slate. Knowing how much money I spent on my college degree, I am so frustrated with twenty-two-year-old me throwing away my opportunity to make the most of my classes. Regurgitating information a few hours later is one thing, but true learning requires *rest.*

A team of researchers at the University of Pennsylvania found that "as the brain cycles through slow-wave and rapid-eye movement (REM) sleep, which happens about five times a night, the hippocampus teaches the neocortex what it learned, transforming novel, fleeting information into enduring memory."[7] If we really want to absorb information and be transformed as we learn, getting sufficient rest is the only way to do it.

Spiritually speaking, worship is that rest. Worship is the rest day in your training regimen. Worship is the night of sleep after a long day of class. Worship is the way repentance (the discomfort and learning) penetrates your whole life. We embrace the discomfort of conviction and let it bring us to that spiritual high of closeness with God, but for that experience to change us, we seek God in worship.

I grew up knowing that Sabbath rest is important and commanded by God. One of the most important things I didn't understand is how God commanded the ancient Israelites to keep the Sabbath by not doing any kind of work (including basic cooking!) on that day (which took place on Saturdays for the ancient Israelites and still for Jewish people today). He also commanded the Israelites to go to the temple to worship three times a year. Many modern Christians observe the principle of Sabbath rest on Sunday, and our temple is the church we go to for worship. As a child, I found this alleged day of rest was anything but. I remember waking up early, bickering with my family, and being bored nearly to tears during the service. After the service, we stopped stressing about church and started stressing about the new week ahead. How did God expect us to honor this commandment to rest on the Sabbath and go to church on the same day?

Friend, worship is the rest. Worship seals in our hearts all the good work God is up to. Worship takes the head knowledge we accumulate and the emotional experiences we cherish, and it integrates them with our physical bodies. As with physical exercise, we won't ever grow and change if we don't embrace the spiritual rest of worship. Eventually I came to understand that the Sabbath wasn't a command to go to the temple; the Sabbath was a command to rest in worship.

And just as rest protects our physical bodies, the rest we encounter in worship is a safeguard for our souls. Have you ever had a night or two of sleeplessness, then found yourself inevitably fighting a cold? When you feel a tickle in your throat and ache in your head, you intuitively know that your body needs an early bedtime to help fight the coming illness. If worship is rest, it offers that same protection to our hearts. If you want to increase your resistance against all the infections going around this dark world, you cannot expect to grow stronger without regularly engaging in worship. As worship resets you to focus on the things of heaven and the victory already won, it reorients you to the reality of those things—to the truth. Many of us seek idols over God because our sense of reality has been warped by living only according to what we can easily see and perceive. When we encounter God in worship, we tell ourselves the truth.

Do you see? Revival is a posture of trusting, nonanxious, culture-shifting rest before the God who never ceases pursuing you. It's a full realization and embrace of the reality of God's relentless *khesed* love for you. That moment when you see your situation clearly and you set aside all the false avenues to peace, joy, and abundance in favor of the real thing. When you truly encounter rest, you can't be anything but revived. Revival is not a movement or an outbreak of emotion (though both often follow); revival is the way you live when you know true, divinely ordained, running-after-you rest.

Isn't it spectacular that Jesus calls us to run toward Him, the source of our rest (and subsequent revival)? Hebrews 12:1–2 says, "Therefore, since we are surrounded by such a great cloud of witnesses, let us throw off everything that hinders and the sin that so easily entangles. And let us run with perseverance the race marked out for us, fixing our eyes on Jesus, the pioneer and perfecter of faith."

Everything else in this world mandates our depletion. We spend our lives trying to possess things that simultaneously try to possess us. We give forty-plus hours of our lives each week in exchange for financial security, and often much more for much less in pursuit of some version of life that revolves around materialism. We sacrifice our physical and mental well-being to look like we'll never age. We change and lose ourselves in relationships with people who will never be able to heal the gaping wounds we've been carrying around. Every other thing we run toward will eventually cost us our lives.

But running toward Jesus? When you respond to His pursuit by pursuing Him, you find yourself stronger, fuller, healthier, and whole. When you lose your life to Him, you truly find it (John 12:25). In this utterly wild reversal found in total dependence on Jesus, the path that looked too daunting for your legs to run becomes straight and smooth.

> Do you not know?
>   Have you not heard?
> The Lord is the everlasting God,
>   the Creator of the ends of the earth.
> He will not grow tired or weary,
>   and his understanding no one can fathom.
> He gives strength to the weary
>   and increases the power of the weak.
> Even youths grow tired and weary,
>   and young men stumble and fall;
> but those who hope in the Lord
>   will renew their strength.
> They will soar on wings like eagles;
>   they will run and not grow weary,
>   they will walk and not be faint. (Isaiah 40:28–31)

What is this if not the revival that your tired and weak body and soul need? Right now. Today. In Jesus, and in no one and nothing else, we find our vitality enriched and renewed. If God's steadfast love gets the final word, where does that leave us? Confident. At rest. Revived. Revival is not an action or an event, but a posture of rest before the living God. To see God's mercy at work is to "live beneath [His] shadow . . . flourish as a garden" (Hosea 14:7 NRSV). When we allow the truth of His pursuit—the truth of the gospel—to sink into our every cell through worship, revival is what we will find.

In his *Confessions*, Augustine writes: "You have made us for yourself, O Lord, and our hearts are restless until they rest in You."[8] Let us not be content with any form of counterfeit rest or peace; let us wrestle deeply with restlessness until we find ourselves revived at the feet of Jesus. Let us encounter radical, culture-shifting revival at His feet in worship of the God who pursues us.

CHAPTER 12

DESIRE MOVED TO ITS FEET

A regular chapel service at Asbury Theological Seminary turned into a weeklong worship service. Hundreds of students worshiped for hours in holy reverence. Thousands traveled from all over the world to the tiny college town of Wilmore, Kentucky, to see what all the fuss was about. I was gripped by the stories I heard about lives rededicated to Christ as well as hearts and bodies healed. During an immensely challenging time to be in ministry, or even just committed to the church, I found myself relieved to hear fresh stories about God moving in the world. Because he started his ministry career as a college pastor, Tanner seriously considered driving to Kentucky to see the Asbury revival for himself, hoping to experience an outpouring of the Holy Spirit.

Almost immediately after word got out about the revival, opinions started swirling around, especially on social media. "This isn't a real revival," some said. "Revival looks like *x*, *y*, and *z*!" Others said things like "The presence of God is in Asbury," as if the presence of God were somehow lesser in their own communities—as if Asbury had gotten a larger portion of an infinite pie and didn't leave enough for the rest of us. Then there were rumors: "The speaker didn't preach the full gospel because he didn't explain the doctrine of sin effectively, and thus it is impossible that this is a true revival."

Distant opinions, formed from secondhand accounts and laced with personal baggage and denominational biases, all converged online at the same time and expected to have the final word on whether a spiritual revival was truly taking place among the students at Asbury.

Under all this discussion was the big question: Is this a real revival?

Plenty of people have lists of what revival means and looks like, with boxes that need to be checked. But I was confused about why we thought our opinions mattered so much. If people encountered the presence of God in a way that transformed them, why is that not enough to label it as revival? If God is truly the "consuming fire" that Deuteronomy 4:24 calls Him, is it worthwhile to try to systematize, predict, and quantify the wildfire as it burns?

I appreciated the thoughtful response from Asbury Theological Seminary's president at the time, Dr. Timothy Tennent, who was reticent to officially label this event as a revival:

> Despite the endless coverage in social media and the regular media which is calling this a revival, I think it is wise to see this, at the current phase, as an awakening. Only if we see lasting transformation which shakes the comfortable foundations of the church and truly brings us all to a new and deeper place can we look back in hindsight and say, "Yes, this has been a revival."[1]

Revival is only as real as the transformation that follows.

Many people think salvation starts and stops with a single quick prayer, a moment of dedicating your life to Jesus. We forget what revival looks like: To the one brought back from the dead, every single relationship, activity, and movement is transformed.

There's a beautiful poem by Lawrence Tribble called "Awaken" that my husband quotes frequently. Tribble wrote it in response to the Great Awakening in the 1700s, and it articulates what revival looks like:

> One man awake,
> Awakens another.
> The second awakens
> His next door brother.
> The three awake can rouse a town
> By turning the whole place
> Upside down.
>
> The many awake
> Can cause such a fuss

It finally awakens the rest of us.
One man up,
With dawn in his eyes
Surely then
Multiplies.[2]

Awakened people awaken others. That is the proof of revival. When you are truly revived by the Holy Spirit, you become forever committed to the revival of others. If there is one thing I hope you take away from this book, it's that God's pursuit of us is not just some vague spiritual reality, but rather a holistic—spiritual, physical, emotional, and intellectual—rescue mission that we, in turn, are meant to live out *holistically*.

True revival, in our churches and in our world, won't just look like people returning to church pews or massive days-long worship services (although I am not denying the validity of these events being part of the revival process). It won't look like a bunch of clean-cut people with perfect church attendance who know all the big theological words and vote for the so-called right people and right policies. If revival is the result of resting in God's pursuit of us, revival will look like revived people pursuing others with goodness and mercy. It will look like proclaiming the gospel in word, yes, but in deed perhaps even more.

I want to be clear: My definition of revival isn't divorced from the historical use of this term as far as the church is concerned. If anything, I'm just putting a finer biblical point on it and tying a stronger historical connection to a word that we've thrown around a lot in recent years. If you're not familiar, the church has seen a number of revivals that not only led to the spiritual salvation of millions but changed the course of all history through a renewed commitment of those saved souls to the idea of "on earth as it is in heaven" (Matthew 6:10). A true understanding of the gospel (i.e., God's pursuit) necessarily ignites a holy fire in the surrounding culture. This fire proclaims "good news to the poor . . . freedom for the prisoners and recovery of sight for the blind," as well as freedom for the oppressed (Luke 4:18). That's precisely what Jesus proclaimed and precisely what Jesus embodied: desire moved to its feet for His beloved.

One of the better-known revivals in history was the Great Awakening, which took place in England and the thirteen colonies in the mid-1700s. From this cultural moment emerged Jonathan Edwards, known largely for his famous sermon "Sinners in the Hands of an Angry God," which is often studied as an illustration of Puritan theology and early American religious attitudes. In this sermon, he said,

> So that, thus it is that natural men are held in the hand of God, over the pit of hell; they have deserved the fiery pit, and are already sentenced to it; and God is dreadfully provoked, his anger is as great towards them as to those that are actually suffering the executions of the fierceness of his wrath in hell, and they have done nothing in the least to appease or abate that anger. . . . Therefore, let every one that is out of Christ, now awake and fly from the wrath to come. The wrath of Almighty God is now undoubtedly hanging over a great part

> of this congregation. Let every one fly out of Sodom: "Haste and escape for your lives, look not behind you, escape to the mountain, lest you be consumed."[3]

Edwards is known for this fire-and-brimstone messaging, which undeniably capitalized on the fear of eternal damnation to urge his hearers to take moral piety seriously and pursue holiness as the only alternative to hell and its destruction. While Edwards's passionate and vivid accounts of life apart from God are uncomfortable to read, they're biblically grounded. This man was deeply passionate about saving souls from eternal separation from God. Many Christians today might find his direct, impassioned way of speaking a necessary response to cultural sins.

Yet Jonathan Edwards knew that this revival couldn't stop with thousands of new Christians who kept their newfound religious fervor under the proverbial bushel. That same Jonathan Edwards, whom we know as one of the most prolific evangelists and revivalists of all time, also said this:

> If God's people in this land were once brought to abound in such deeds of love, as much as in praying, hearing, singing, and religious meetings and conference, it would be a most blessed omen. Nothing would have a greater tendency to bring the God of love down from heaven to earth; so amiable would be the sight in the eyes of our loving and exalted Redeemer, that it would soon as it were fetch him down from his throne in heaven, to set up his tabernacle with men on the earth, and dwell with them.[4]

Edwards knew that holiness and repentance work in tandem with our witness in the world. The Puritan colonies from which he came were meant to be a "city on a hill," in reference to Matthew 5:14–16:

> "You are the light of the world. A town built on a hill cannot be hidden. Neither do people light a lamp and put it under a bowl. Instead they put it on its stand, and it gives light to everyone in the house. In the same way, let your light shine before others, that they may see your good deeds and glorify your Father in heaven."

Although the Puritans got many things wrong, and although we might disagree with Edwards's delivery, they got this right: We are the light of the world, and our presence in the world must shine that same light to others. Because we reflect the ultimate Light that pursued us in the darkness, our good deeds prove that we have basked in the radiance of God's radical love.

Another phase of the Great Awakening took place in England, and it is known as the Wesleyan revival. John Wesley, known as the father of Methodism, his brother Charles, and the famed evangelist George Whitefield took to the streets of London. At that time, the Church of England was known for its decadence and its ineffectiveness while the rest of society continued to plunge into rampant immorality and crime. These three men spoke in countryside fields or on the city streets; the formal pulpits were not offered to them. Both by design and as a result of where the Wesleys and Whitefield preached, the

Great Awakening in England mostly affected the lower classes—the people most disenfranchised by the English culture that had previously based human worth and dignity on social class. Participants in the Wesleyan movement advocated for fair wages and improved living conditions as the direct outflow of their evangelistic efforts. While this revival began with an effort to convert souls out of the darkness and into the light, it also sought to ensure that those same souls were able to live well in the here and now.

The Wesleyan revival also directly led to the abolition of slavery in England. John Wesley's very last letter was to William Wilberforce, a member of the British Parliament and the man who helped finally abolish the slave trade in England in 1807 after twenty years of fighting for this cause. In that letter, John Wesley wrote, "Go on, in the name of God and in the power of His might, till even American slavery (the vilest that ever saw the sun) shall vanish away before it."[5]

The idea that spiritual revival could somehow occur in isolation from the day-to-day issues of struggling people didn't exist. Not among the most prolific revivalists known to the Western world, and not now. The Great Awakening laid the groundwork that acknowledged all humans are equal before God, a truth that spoke deeply to the needs in that society. When the Second Great Awakening began in the late 1700s in the United States, people in the American South and new frontier communities flocked to receive the gospel in camp meetings.[6] During this time, the growing church launched social movement after social movement, mirroring the spiritual realities they preached from the pulpit in this renewed expression of social life. More than any other, this revival movement affected secular living, simply through the myriad reforms and initiatives that sprang from it. Missionary societies formed to bring about the same type of revival around the world, and these same missionary societies funded the construction of schools and hospitals globally. Similarly, efforts to circulate spiritual literature and start Bible studies abounded.

Another example is the temperance movement, which was a direct result of American revivalist Charles Finney's belief that a true awakening in the United States had to involve an outer expression of holiness and a socially involved church. It wasn't perfect. The point is that, once again, the revival of the Second Great Awakening was inherently and inextricably tied to Christians being willing to take an active role in promoting the good of their neighbors. Particularly on the issue of slavery, "Charles Finney felt that part of the difficulty in achieving abolition in America was that this crusade was running ahead of the evangelizing of the nation, whereas abolition should be made 'an appendage of a general revival of religion.'"[7] For Finney, revival fueled the abolitionist cause, but slavery would finally meet its end only through a true understanding of the gospel.

Perhaps just as Finney feared, the Social Gospel movement—a progressive movement of the late nineteenth and early twentieth centuries that held that biblical principles should be applied to social problems to solve them effectively—ultimately prioritized social issues over theological and spiritual ones.[8]

Rather than a holistic gospel that is primarily spiritual and yet necessarily tangible, the social gospel downplayed doctrine and contextualized the whole gospel through the lens of modern social issues rather than the supernatural battle described in Ephesians 6:10–17. Likewise, Prohibition was just one social movement among many that was misguided in its efforts to reform society along so-called holy lines. Not all social effects of the Second Great Awakening were theologically correct or positive.

However, the revivalists of this era understood that "the Old Testament prophets habitually called for a threefold repentance on the part of God's people: the rejection of idolatry or false religion; the renunciation of adultery, drunkenness and other personal sins; and a renewal of caring for the poor and needy, forsaking indifference, fighting oppression and seeking justice."[9] They called for a collective rejection of immorality and sin, a personal kind of repentance, and the desire to make concerted, organized efforts to care for the disenfranchised and oppressed of their day.

Perhaps you've heard of the Azusa Street Revival. Preacher William Joseph Seymour arrived in Los Angeles in 1906 to become the pastor of a small church, only to be prohibited from preaching there due to his bold style and claims about the power of the Holy Spirit. Undeterred, Seymour started hosting prayer meetings that exploded into huge services, with so much growth that the gathering relocated to a new building on—you guessed it!—Azusa Street. This gathering, unlike the previous well-known revivals in American history, was not only led by a Black man well before the civil rights movement of the 1960s but also marked by racial diversity in a time when this was scandalous to many.

The Azusa Street Revival is often considered the beginning of Pentecostalism, but aside from that, "so many missionaries spread the word from Azusa that within two years the movement had spread to over fifty nations."[10] The Azusa revival, like all the rest, grew legs and went out to draw more people in. Even today, the Pentecostal church continues to grow (while most denominations' numbers are plummeting): "The Assemblies of God (AG), the world's largest Pentecostal denomination, has enjoyed sustained growth for decades, growing 51% in the same time period in which the UCC [United Church of Christ] and PCUSA [Presbyterian Church (USA)] declined by a near-identical percentage."[11] It's projected that there will be over one billion Pentecostals worldwide in the next thirty-five years. Pentecostal missionaries lead the world in the number of conversions each year.[12] In crossing racial lines as well as focusing intensely on a personal experience with the Holy Spirit, the revival on Azusa Street extended beyond its initial events and, to this day, continues to cross cultural lines and draw people into God's work in the world.

When the Holy Spirit fell on the apostles at Pentecost (Acts 2), they experienced the Holy Spirit in a whole new way. They spoke in tongues they didn't know, such that people from an array of other nations could understand the message in their own languages (verses 5–11). This outpouring of the Holy Spirit looked foolish to some, who thought the disciples were like a bunch of adults drunk at nine in the morning. This spectacle allowed Peter to share the whole gospel in the context of the history of Israel, and we are told that three thousand received the gospel that day.

But don't miss this: A following set of verses gives us a clear, specific picture of living in a community of the renewed and in fellowship with those similarly transformed by the Holy Spirit:

> They devoted themselves to the apostles' teaching and to fellowship, to the breaking of bread and to prayer. Everyone was filled with awe at the many wonders and signs performed by the apostles. All the believers were together and had everything in common. They sold property and possessions to give to anyone who had need. Every day they continued to meet together in the temple courts. They broke bread in their homes and ate together with glad and sincere hearts, praising God and enjoying the favor of all the people. And the Lord added to their number daily those who were being saved. (Acts 2:42–47)

If you know what happened after the initial revival at Azusa, you are likely aware that it ultimately fractured and split due to internal conflict and external pressures. But it wasn't like that in the early church of Acts: The revival drew them together and enabled them to live in radical community and joyful sharing. In turn, this community compelled even more converts to join their movement. The revival was grounded in a community that stood against every selfish human impulse and freed its members to experience true togetherness.

Perhaps the best-known modern revivalist in America is Billy Graham, who had this to say about revival: "No nation has ever improved morally without a spiritual revival. History proves that point. Various nations of the past have tried to improve and pick themselves up by their bootstraps morally in order to save their country from disintegration, but they could not do it unless they experienced a religious revival."[13] The converse is also true: No nation that experiences a spiritual revival can help but also experience a subsequent social renewal. Although Billy Graham is well-known for his crusades that filled stadiums and saved millions, he also pioneered the Lausanne Movement alongside John Stott. This organization is committed to fulfilling the Great Commission (Matthew 28:19). John Stott served as the chief architect of the Lausanne Movement's mission statement, known as the Lausanne Covenant. Article 5, "Christian Social Responsibility," states in part:

> We affirm that God is both the Creator and the judge of all men. We therefore should share his concern for justice and reconciliation throughout human society and for the liberation of men and women from every kind of oppression. . . . Although reconciliation with other people is not reconciliation with God, nor is social action evangelism, nor is political liberation salvation, nevertheless we affirm that evangelism and sociopolitical involvement are both part of our Christian duty. For both are necessary expressions of our doctrines of God and Man, our love for our neighbour and our obedience to Jesus

> Christ. . . . The salvation we claim should be transforming us in the totality of our personal and social responsibilities. Faith without works is dead.[14]

In a time when social action and biblical inerrancy are often pitted against each other in the context of political debate, I want all of us to really meditate on these words that are not so far removed from modern American evangelical conceptions of truth. They're not from English Presbyterians in the 1700s or from Baptist preachers in Appalachia in the 1800s. Perhaps the discussion about the Azusa Street Revival made you a little nervous (depending on your own denominational or theological leanings). But the Lausanne Covenant has a direct stamp of approval from America's pastor, Billy Graham.

As people renewed and redeemed, we are commanded to go into the world with this good news that changes hearts and transforms lives, both spiritually and physically. It makes total sense that Billy Graham, with his heart set on the revival of America, was familiar with the reality that revival releases us into action for the sake of the world.

> How beautiful on the mountains
>   are the feet of those who bring good news,
> who proclaim peace,
>   who bring good tidings,
>   who proclaim salvation,
> who say to Zion,
>   "Your God reigns!" (Isaiah 52:7)

There is certainly no shortage of criticism for any of these revival movements or the people they involve. But the point is this: Not one single revival in recorded history was limited to a detached, transcendent version of salvation. In every case, conversion begets some form of social transformation. In every case, those who encounter the love of Jesus run away from comfort and toward adversity (in whatever form) for the sake of other lost souls. They change policies and build schools. They fund hospitals and provide meals. They go to hostile environments and people who hate them, and they offer sacrificial love and aid. They pursue other people the way God pursued them. When revived and restored followers of Jesus are set loose on a dark and dying world, transformation happens.

Revival is not just a spiritual thing, nor only physical, nor only personal. Revival engages human beings holistically, both in their salvation and in the transformation of their will to go and share the gospel with others.

Jesus the Messiah, who conquered death and hades to deliver us to heaven, announced Himself in words that draw from an Old Testament prophecy:

> "The Spirit of the Lord is on me,
> because he has anointed me
> to proclaim good news to the poor.
> He has sent me to proclaim freedom for the prisoners
> and recovery of sight for the blind,
> to set the oppressed free,
> to proclaim the year of the Lord's favor."
> (Luke 4:18–19, quoting Isaiah 61:1–2)

We pray for revival in these dark days, but I wonder: Do we truly want the kind of revival that God brings? Do we really want to partner with Christ in this huge and difficult mission? As the aroma of Christ in the world (2 Corinthians 2:15), do we want to bear good news to poor people, maybe out on the street in front of our homes? Do we desire to see prisoners, maybe even criminals who wronged us, set free when they earnestly repent? Do we want the blind to regain their sight and thus see all the ways that we Jesus followers have been complicit in the exploitation of those who are powerless against it? Do we want to be the prophetic voice calling out the oppressors as we announce this freedom?

It's important to acknowledge that sharing the full gospel is a fearsome thing. The oppressors in our world don't want the interference, not the spiritual interference we can't see or the human interference we can. The gospel is life and peace and fresh breath to those who are in bondage, but it is a harsh proclamation of guilt to anyone who participated in fashioning those chains. You will offend across the usual party lines, and you will never—not a day before Jesus returns—go an hour without your renewed gospel eyes detecting the kind of darkness that needs illumination.

Isn't sharing the gospel all about saving souls, about people accepting Jesus and His sacrifice and making Him Lord over their lives? Yes. The life, death, and resurrection of Jesus are everything. They change *everything.* They change everything about us. They make us citizens of a kingdom we can't see and agents of change in a world that doesn't want us (John 15:18). We won't get to feel at home (Hebrews 13:14). Jesus's pursuit of us and our submission to Him transform us into people who pursue gospel transformation in others and for others with every fiber of our being. But we don't do it alone. The Holy Spirit will empower us to say yes to the brutality and supernaturality of that calling every morning, if we will let Him.

My heart is grieved for the church I know well, and for the way we have abdicated our God-given role of bringing life and freedom to every person and every space, not in addition to but *because of* the gospel. We like social action when it benefits us or protects our priorities. We, like Peter, are quick to take up the sword and quick to go on the defensive. But are we willing to jump into action as quickly for the cruciform call to seek others' good at our *own* expense?

We will not see true culture-shifting revival until we embrace the truth that it will require us to go to tough places to pursue people we don't like, with ways more loving than we'd choose. But a Christian who has turned from sin and found rest in God's relentless, steadfast love and pursuit can't imagine anything else but saying yes to God's call to love his neighbor as himself. And we can do this knowing we're not doing any of it on our own. When God draws near—which He does in His pursuit of us, His people—He will set right every injustice, and He will satisfy every hunger.

Revelation paints a picture of God's redemptive work, already begun yet still in progress:

> "Look! God's dwelling place is now among the people, and he will dwell with them. They will be his people, and God

> himself will be with them and be their God. 'He will wipe every tear from their eyes. There will be no more death' or mourning or crying or pain, for the old order of things has passed away." (Revelation 21:3–4)

Find rest in knowing that God is near and pursuing your heart, both to bring you ultimate salvation and to offer you "life . . . to the full" (John 10:10) today. Even if you are in the wilderness, know that He is too. You will see that His goodness and mercy have followed you. He is calling you back to who you are. Find rest in the joy of knowing that God wants to be near you. Be revived in that rest. From there, offer Him worship and go forth, illuminating every space you're in with His light.

ACKNOWLEDGMENTS

For their support, encouragement, and wisdom, I owe a huge debt of gratitude to the following people:

Tanner, my husband. For walking through this whole story by my side and for refusing to turn away from me, even when you probably should have. Thank you for the way you have never complained about the unbalanced workload that falls on you when I have a big deadline. Thank you for running your own ministry while simultaneously and wholeheartedly supporting mine. Most of all, thank you for (unsurprisingly) being the kind of father who will make it easy for our children to believe that God is absolutely crazy about them.

To my babies, Judah, Thea, and Shepherd. Because I look at your sweet little faces and I need you to know that God's goodness and mercy are always pursuing you. That, more than anything else, gave me the energy to get this book done.

My mom, Amy. Your artist soul and way with words paved an easy path for me to believe that writing a book was something I could do. Thank you for being faithful to every fire that the Lord has put in your heart.

My dad, Bill. For your tenderness and humor. I know that if I call you for help, you will always show up. The older I get, the more I realize how rare that is.

Haley, my sister. For being present on the hard days and for not judging me when I was a little too honest.

To Bob and Mary Howey, my beloved grandparents. Your lives set a legacy of faith into motion, and it is because of your answered prayers that I am walking with Jesus now.

To the friends who sent late-night pep-talk texts to keep me going when I was exhausted and flowers to help me remember to celebrate the wins. Having you in my corner is an undeserved gift.

Thank you to Keren Baltzer and the Zondervan team, who offered unending wisdom and patience, all the while affirming that this message matters. You are so good at your work, and I have been blessed by it.

My Jesus. You have pursued my heart through the wilderness, and You have been kind to restore each and every gift I have carelessly thrown away. Let this book accomplish precisely what You have ordained. I am undone by Your goodness to me.

NOTES

Introduction

1. "Marry a Prostitute!," Fuller Theological Seminary, accessed January 20, 2025, https://www.fuller.edu/next-faithful-step/resources/marry-a-prostitute/.

Chapter 1: Surely His Goodness Will Follow Me

1. John Piper, host, *Ask Pastor John*, podcast, episode 1579, "Why Did God Create Us?," Desiring God, January 25, 2021, https://www.desiringgod.org/interviews/why-did-god-create-us.
2. "Enki and Ninmah: Translation," in *The Electronic Text Corpus of Sumerian Literature*, ed. Jeremy Black et al., University of Oxford, May 14, 1999, https://etcsl.orinst.ox.ac.uk/section1/tr112.htm.
3. "Tony Campolo Throws a Party for a Prostitute," Preaching Today, June 2008, https://www.preachingtoday.com/illustrations/2008/june/15742.html.

Chapter 2: For His Name's Sake

1. Michael Reeves, "God's Love," in *Overflow: How the Joy of the Trinity Inspires Our Mission* (Chicago: Moody Publishers, 2021), 16.
2. Jeremy Weber, "Six Surprises from Bono's Interview with Focus on the Family," *Christianity Today*, June 21, 2013, https://www.christianitytoday.com/2013/06/bono-interview-with-focus-on-family-jim-daly/.
3. Martin Luther, *Luther's Works*, vol. 31, *Career of the Reformer I*, ed. Jaroslav Jan Pelikan, Hilton C. Oswald, and Helmut T. Lehmann (Philadelphia: Fortress Press, 1999).

Chapter 3: The Lion That Saves

1. CPS Psychosocial Paediatrics Committee, "Effective Discipline: A Healthy Approach," *Paediatrics & Child Health* 9, no. 1 (January 1, 2004): 43–44, https://academic.oup.com/pch/article/9/1/43/2648486.
2. C. S. Lewis, *The Lion, the Witch and the Wardrobe* (New York: HarperTrophy, 2005), 86.

Chapter 4: When It Feels Like God Has Given Up

1. Glenn Packiam, *Discover the Mystery of Faith: How Worship Shapes Believing* (Colorado Springs: David C Cook, 2013), 20.
2. "Prescribed Fire," US Forest Service, US Department of Agriculture, accessed June 18, 2024, https://www.fs.usda.gov/managing-land/prescribed-fire.

Chapter 5: Freedom in His Net

1. Sam Peltzman, "The Socio Political Demography of Happiness," Working Paper No. 331 (George J. Stigler Center for the Study of the Economy and the State, University of Chicago, July 12, 2023), SSRN, https://papers.ssrn.com/sol3/papers.cfm?abstract_id=4508123.
2. Timothy Keller, *Making Sense of God: An Invitation to the Skeptical* (New York: Viking Books, 2016), 116–17.

3. "Residential Design Award of Honor: Magnolia River Ranch," ASLA 2006 Student Awards, American Society of Landscape Architects, accessed June 22, 2024, https://www.asla.org/awards/2006/studentawards/282.html.

Chapter 6: You Are Wanted

1. Philip Ryken, *The Love of Loves in the Song of Songs* (Wheaton, IL: Crossway, 2019), 36.
2. John Schloss, "Conflict Between the Sons of Ishmael and Isaac," Trinium Newsletter, American University of Health Sciences, October 27, 2023, https://news.auhs.edu/conflict-between-the-sons-of-ishmael-and-isaac/.

Chapter 7: Pursued by the God Who Provides

1. Erika Barba-Müller et al., "Brain Plasticity in Pregnancy and the Postpartum Period: Links to Maternal Caregiving and Mental Health," *Archives of Women's Mental Health* 22, no. 2 (April 2019): 289–99, https://pubmed.ncbi.nlm.nih.gov/30008085/.

Chapter 8: Darkness Doesn't Stand a Chance

1. "See a Victory," by Elevation Worship, produced by Elevation Worship, released as a single on August 9, 2019.
2. Paul Sutter, "What Is the Most Distant Thing We Can See?," Space.com, March 21, 2024, https://www.space.com/what-is-the-most-distant-thing-we-can-see.

Chapter 9: Boundaries That Bear With

1. Henry Cloud and John Townsend, *Boundaries: When to Say Yes, How to Say No to Take Control of Your Life* (Grand Rapids: Zondervan, 2002), 34.
2. Helen Carefoot, "Why the Misuse of 'Boundaries' to Control Other People Is an Especially Harmful Kind of Manipulation," Well+Good, July 12, 2023, https://www.wellandgood.com/misuse-boundaries/.

3. This phrase is attributed to Nicholas Wolterstorff; see Nicholas Wolterstorff, *Justice: Rights and Wrongs* (Princeton, NJ: Princeton University Press, 2008).
4. *Merriam-Webster*, "ghosting," accessed July 12, 2024, https://www.merriam-webster.com/dictionary/ghosting.

Chapter 10: Mutual Pursuit

1. "What Does It Mean to Sin?," BibleProject, March 15, 2018, 5 min., 43 sec., https://bibleproject.com/explore/video/khata-sin/.
2. Sam Storms, "The Christian and Repentance," The Gospel Coalition, January 14, 2020, https://www.thegospelcoalition.org/essay/the-christian-and-repentance/.
3. Dallas Willard, *The Divine Conspiracy: Rediscovering Our Hidden Life in God* (New York: HarperOne, 2018), 243.
4. Christian Smith and Melinda Lundquist Denton, *Soul Searching: The Religious and Spiritual Lives of American Teenagers* (New York: Oxford University Press, 2009).

Chapter 11: Revival from Rest

1. Springtide, "Gen Z and Religion—What the Statistics Say," Springtide Research Institute, September 29, 2022, https://springtideresearch.org/post/religion-and-spirituality/gen-z-and-religion-what-the-statistics-say.
2. *Merriam-Webster*, "revive," accessed November 6, 2024, https://www.merriam-webster.com/dictionary/revive.
3. Tim Keller, "'Lord, Do It Again': Tim Keller on Revival," The Gospel Coalition, March 17, 2023, https://www.thegospelcoalition.org/article/tim-keller-revival/; Timothy Keller, "Revival: Ways and Means," TimothyKeller.com, January 10, 2011, https://timothykeller.com/blog/2011/1/10/revival-ways-and-means.
4. Brian C. Tefft, "Drowsy Driving in Fatal Crashes, United States, 2017–2021," AAA Foundation for Traffic Safety, March 2024, https://aaafoundation.org/drowsy-driving-in-fatal-crashes-united-states-2017-2021/.

5. James K. A. Smith, *You Are What You Love: The Spiritual Power of Habit* (Grand Rapids: Brazos Press, 2016), 77.
6. Wayne L. Westcott, "Resistance Training Is Medicine: Effects of Strength Training on Health," *Current Sports Medicine Reports* 11, no. 4 (2012): 209–16, https://pubmed.ncbi.nlm.nih.gov/22777332/.
7. Michele W. Berger, "During Sleep, One Brain Region Teaches Another, Converting Novel Data into Enduring Memories," Penn Today, October 24, 2022, https://penntoday.upenn.edu/news/Penn-research-during-sleep-one-brain-region-teaches-another-memory-formation.
8. Augustine, *Confessions* 1.1–2, 1.5 (CSEL 33), cited in "Our Heart Is Restless Until It Rests in You – Augustine," Crossroads Initiative, July 1, 2021, https://www.crossroadsinitiative.com/media/articles/ourheartisrestlessuntilitrestsinyou/.

Chapter 12: Desire Moved to Its Feet

1. Timothy Tennent, "Thoughts on the Asbury Awakening," TimothyTennent.com, February 14, 2023, https://timothytennent.com/thoughts-on-the-asbury-awakening/.
2. Lawrence Tribble, "Awaken," in *A Patriot's Handbook: Songs, Poems, Stories, and Speeches Celebrating the Land We Love*, ed. Caroline Kennedy (New York: Grand Central Publishing, 2016), Kindle.
3. Jonathan Edwards, "Sinners in the Hands of an Angry God," July 8, 1741, Enfield, CT, sermon transcript, Blue Letter Bible, May 1, 2014, https://www.blueletterbible.org/Comm/edwards_jonathan/Sermons/Sinners.cfm.
4. Quoted in Richard F. Lovelace, *Dynamics of Spiritual Life: An Evangelical Theology of Renewal* (Downers Grove, IL: IVP Academic, 2020), 207.
5. "Wesley, Wilberforce and the Battle Against Slavery," Methodist Church Resource Hub, accessed July 23, 2024, https://www.methodist.org.uk/for-churches/resources/posts/wesley-wilberforce-and-the-battle-against-slavery/.

6. *Britannica*, "Second Great Awakening," last updated December 17, 2024, https://www.britannica.com/topic/Second-Great-Awakening. See also Adriaan C. Neele, "The Dawn of Missionary Societies," *Tabletalk*, May 2019, https://tabletalkmagazine.com/article/2019/05/dawn-missionary-societies/.
7. Lovelace, *Dynamics of Spiritual Life*, 202.
8. *Encyclopedia of Christianity in the United States*, "Social Gospel – Timeline Movement," ARDA, https://www.thearda.com/us-religion/history/timelines/entry?etype=3&eid=46.
9. Lovelace, *Dynamics of Spiritual Life*, 202.
10. "A Glimpse of the Kingdom of Heaven: The Azusa Street Revival," PBS series This Far by Faith, 2003, https://www.pbs.org/thisfarbyfaith/journey_3/p_9.html.
11. Ed Stetzer, "Pentecostals: How Do They Keep Growing While Other Groups Are Declining?," ChurchLeaders.com, June 27, 2023, https://churchleaders.com/voices/453879-pentecostals-how-do-they-keep-growing.html.
12. Elle Hardy, "Inside the Fastest Growing Religious Movement on Earth," *Premier Christianity*, January 27, 2022, https://www.premierchristianity.com/features/inside-the-fastest-growing-religious-movement-on-earth/6009.article.
13. Billy Graham, "Billy Graham: Revival or Disintegration," Billy Graham Evangelistic Association of Canada, May 12, 2021, https://www.billygraham.ca/stories/billy-graham-revival-or-disintegration/.
14. John Stott, The Lausanne Covenant (1974; repr., Lausanne Movement, 2012), https://lausanne.org/statement/lausanne-covenant#christian-social-responsibility.

Set Your Eyes Higher

A 40-Day Reset to Slow Your Anxiety and Fix Your Focus on God (A Devotional)

Whitney Lowe

Life feeling out of control? Overwhelmed and need a break? You're invited to a forty-day reset that will help you let go of what's not serving you and turn your gaze toward a God who loves you. *Set Your Eyes Higher* is a life-changing devotional journey from anxiety to peace.

We spend a lot of time looking down. Mostly at our phones. Sometimes at ourselves. The artificial blue light in our eyes makes us anxious about the world. It makes us chase trends that have nothing to do with who we want to be. It causes us to put time, energy, and brain space into what won't last.

It's time to look up. Each daily devotion in *Set Your Eyes Higher* includes honest reflections, a suggested Scripture reading, and a prayer that will help you refocus your attention on God. This insightful guide for our modern world will help you if you are:

- Searching for a rhythm to anchor your spiritual practices
- Looking to take control of your time and gain clarity on what you want in life
- Seeking long-lasting contentment over trends
- Wanting to let go of the world's worries you are carrying on your shoulders

Set Your Eyes Higher will help you find new perspective, purpose, power, and peace. If you're feeling unmoored because you've taken your eyes off what matters most, the hope you seek is within reach—if you're ready to look up.

Available in stores and online!

From the Publisher

GREAT BOOKS

ARE EVEN BETTER WHEN THEY'RE SHARED!

Help other readers find this one

- Post a review at your favorite online bookseller
- Post a picture on a social media account and share why you enjoyed it
- Send a note to a friend who would also love it—or better yet, give them a copy

Thanks for reading!